PRAISE FOR
CITY OF MAN, KINGDOM OF GOD

In a culture where it is popular to rebel against authority, *City of Man, Kingdom of God* provides an important reminder that the Scripture demands believers to submit to government, including bad ones. At the same time, Johnson reminds us that such authority is not absolute. This book is a thought-provoking, clear, and necessary read, especially in a society where believers are wrestling through how to interact with a government that is becoming increasingly hostile to Christian belief and practice.

> — **Abner Chou, PhD**
> President and John F. MacArthur Endowed Fellow, The Master's University

Since 2020, we have all had a crash course in how Christians should relate to government. Pastor Jesse Johnson has written a book that captures those hard-learned biblical lessons that will benefit generations to come. Johnson recovers the Puritan understanding of government and shows why it matters today. It is a much-needed reminder that as we render unto Caesar what is his, we must not forget to render to God what belongs to him.

> — **Austin Duncan**
> Associate Pastor,
> Grace Community Church, Los Angeles

CITY OF MAN, KINGDOM OF GOD

CITY OF MAN, KINGDOM OF GOD

WHY CHRISTIANS RESPECT, OBEY, AND RESIST GOVERNMENT

Jesse Johnson

Edited by Michael T. Hamilton

DEDICATION

To the courageous Christians at Immanuel Bible Church
who, in the summer of 2020, by God's grace and providence, were able to live out the truths in this book.

CONTENTS

INTRODUCTION

A BETTER WAY
FOR CHRISTIANS TO
UNDERSTAND GOVERNMENT

For [government] is God's servant for your good.

— Romans 13:4

For kingship belongs to Yahweh, and he rules over all nations.

— Psalm 22:28

The COVID-19 pandemic turned American churches upside down and inside out. In a culture that had long prided itself on religious liberty, churches were suddenly closed by mandate. Congregations that had so frequently begun their services by praying "Thank you, Lord, for the freedom we have to worship..." found themselves without the legal freedom to do just that.

And few churches knew how to respond.

An ironic truth about COVID-19 is that for most of its victims, the ultimate cause of death was not the virus itself but rather underlying health issues that were merely exacerbated by it. News reports sometimes distinguished

11

between dying *from* COVID-19 and dying *with* COVID-19. Most, it seemed, were dying *with* the virus. Americans even learned a new medical term—*comorbidity*.[1] The virus didn't cause a person's health issues, but the virus certainly exposed and inflamed them, often creating a lethal combination.

The concept of COVID-19 comorbidities was true for churches as well. As churches shut their doors, some congregations realized just how disconnected they were from their leadership. Those congregations had no way to care for each other outside their normal weekly gathering. Some realized they had no small-group structures and thus were not able to disciple each other effectively when the building was closed. Other churches were not healthy financially before the forced closures, and the pandemic made paying their bills impossible. I am personally aware of some churches that closed, never to reopen. These are examples of church comorbidities. Those churches died *with* the virus, not *of* the virus.

But for me, COVID-19 exposed the most glaring deficiency in the church—one that was not ecclesiological, but *theological.* American Christians lacked a biblical understanding of how churches should relate to government. When American governments—whether city councils or

---

[1] Comorbidity (n) (koe-mor-BID-ih-tee): "Coexistence of two or more disease processes." (Medical Dictionary for the Health Professions and Nursing, s.v. "comorbidity," accessed April 18, 2022, https://medical-dictionary.thefreedictionary.com/comorbidity.)

federal bureaucrats—ordered churches to close, it seemed that too few knew what to do. For the first time in recent memory, American Christians had to recover a robust understanding of how the church should relate to a hostile government.

While this may have been a relatively new question for Christians in the US, it is obviously not a new issue globally. Churches throughout Asia have often been forced to meet secretly. There are nations where being a believer in Christ is against the law. The reality for many believers in those countries is jail time, beatings, and even martyrdom. Followers of Jesus in hostile countries generally have a more robust understanding of how Christians should relate to civil authority.

But in the United States, our view of submission is underdeveloped. American Christians generally believe that they are to "obey the government unless the government commands sin." But what is "sin"? This word is often left undefined. What if the government bans churches from meeting? Or says, "You can meet, but only fifteen people at a time"? Or maybe "only fifty people at a time"? Or maybe "you can meet, but you can't shake hands or sit next to each other or hold hands in prayer or have communion or baptize"? Or, "If you do meet, you cannot sing"?

These were all real examples of edicts given in the last few years. And I don't think anyone would seriously argue that churches were adequately prepared with a robust biblical response. Many didn't seem even to understand the theological questions such prohibitions raised.

IS THE GOVERNMENT GOD?

Most American evangelical churches approached the COVID-19-inspired shutdowns with deference because of their default position, "Obey the government at all times unless it commands you to sin." However, that adage is woefully inadequate and gives government a level of deference that is owed only to God. This is not the historical view of Christians toward government.

But for obvious reasons, that view of government is what has been favored by governments themselves. Political leaders like to think of themselves as being owed absolute obedience, and in their mind, the escape clause "except in cases of sin" is meaningless. After all, they (supposedly) want only what is good for us, and (ostensibly) would never command us to do something evil. Historically, Lutherans and Catholics have generally embraced that view of submission because they have often been well connected politically. When the emperor is appointed by the pope, complete obedience to the government is required.

But what about when the king has declared himself to be the head of the church? This is exactly what happened in England during the English Reformation in the sixteenth and seventeenth centuries. Henry VIII broke from Rome and assumed control of the church in England, soon to be renamed the Church of England. Subsequent British monarchs would insist that only pastors ordained and licensed by the crown were permitted to preach in churches. At the height of persecution, the government even dictated the church liturgy, including what passages could be preached on and what topics could be covered in prayer!

Many pastors opposed these restrictions. Some, like John Bunyan, were imprisoned. Others, like Samuel Rutherford, were condemned to death for their opposition. In 1662, some two thousand pastors resigned their ministry rather than submitting to laws that regulated church worship. Many took to preaching outdoors in fields and plazas, which led to the Five Mile Act (1665), a law that banned preachers from living within five miles of a place they had formerly preached.

The inadequacy of "Obey the government at all times unless it commands you to sin" should be obvious. Is it sinful to move five miles away? Is it sinful to preach on certain passages on certain days? Of course not. But framing the issue in those terms misses the larger and more significant question entirely. The right question to ask is this: *Does the government have the authority to regulate church worship?*

Today's American church seems to have landed with the Lutherans and Catholics, and COVID-19 exposed this reality. Pastors, elders, and entire congregations struggled to come to terms with how to respond to a government that had shuttered their churches. We lacked the theological chops to understand what was happening, and "Obey the government at all times unless it commands you to sin" was revealed to be a woefully inadequate rubric.

CAN YOU 'SOCIAL DISTANCE' AT A RIOT?

COVID-19 was not the only source of social upheaval to affect the church in recent years. Simultaneous with the global pandemic were riots that swept the United States in response to the murder of George Floyd. Beyond the riots, there were massive protests, often targeting law enforcement.

Christians tended to respond negatively to these demonstrations. In many cases, the same government leaders who ordered churches to close took to the streets and joined the protests. Calls to "defund the police" soon became a staple of American culture, and antagonism against law enforcement became politically correct.

It cannot be overstated how culturally schizophrenic this seemed. Churches were closed at the government's order, while society was simultaneously protesting the very law enforcement that would supposedly enforce such an order.

That tension is what this book seeks to address. How should Christians view government, especially when that government is regulating or banning corporate worship? How should Christians respond when society rejects the legitimacy of law enforcement, especially given that some actions of law enforcement are manifestly unjust?

When government does what is right by protecting rights given by God, then it is owed obedience, submission, and honor. But when government violates those rights, Christians are no longer bound to submit to laws that do not serve the purpose for which God made government.

The purpose of this book is to help you navigate these tensions.

In chapter 1, I argue that God designed government, and that he placed particular limits on it. Thus, our freedoms and rights move from God to man and ought to be defended by the government. I will explain the blessings government can bring to the world with a focus on how government—when it is functioning properly—serves as a protection for human society.

In chapter 2, I examine what happens when government oversteps its purpose, and I argue for the Puritan understanding of Romans 13 over and against the Lutheran/Catholic interpretation. I will show that when the government goes too far, Romans 13 tells Christians how to respond and when to obey.

In chapter 3, I explore the concept of justice in society and how Christians should respond to a world where injustice seems ubiquitous. Because our understanding of cause and effect can often be deficient, we easily misdiagnose what is wrong with society. Turning to Ecclesiastes, we find God's word giving practical wisdom for how to interact with wrongs in an upside-down and inside-out world.

In chapter 4, I conclude the book by mapping out the two-kingdom approach to living as a subject of the King of Kings, while also living under the authority of lesser magistrates. Sometimes we are torn about which authority reigns where, and drawing from Jesus's rebuke of the Herodians, I conclude with an appeal to render worship only to God—never to government.

Without understanding from the whole of Scripture (as opposed to a handful of famous verses isolated from context) where our obligations to government start and end, Christians will fall off either edge of the sword: either we will render unto ourselves what is Caesar's, or we will render unto Caesar what is God's.

Only by understanding the boundaries within which God ordained government can we understand our obligations to obey the government and (at times) to resist it. And only then can we, the church, walk in faithfulness to God's revealed purposes for government.

1

GOVERNMENT IN THE BEGINNING

And for your lifeblood I will require a reckoning: from every beast I will require it and from man. From his fellow man I will require a reckoning for the life of man.

> Whoever sheds the blood of man,
> by man shall his blood be shed,
> for God made man in his own image.

And you, be fruitful and multiply, increase greatly on the earth and multiply in it.

— Genesis 9:5–7

Pastoring a church in the Washington, DC, area has given me a front-row seat to this American phenomenon: somehow, every four years, Americans face "the most important election in the history of our country," if not in the history of all Western civilization. Each election cycle we are told that the risks of losing this particular partisan struggle exceed those of the previous election, which was more important than the one before that, and so on.

But is that true? Is every American presidential election more important than the one before it?

The United States has a long history of political division. Ever since the honeymoon period of George Washington's two terms, every presidential election from John Adams to Joe Biden has been cast as a mortal struggle for our country's future and freedom.

As early as 1796, the rhetoric took on doomsday verbiage: *If John Adams loses, our country is over. If Thomas Jefferson wins, the American experiment will fail.* Guess what: Adams won. Somehow the country made it to 1800, and the doomsday campaigns returned, only this time, Jefferson won—we built a monument commemorating him and everything he stood for—and still America has somehow continued into its forty-sixth presidential administration.

Labeling each election "the most important one" reveals how people feel about government. The very nature of democracy gives every American a vote—a voice. Most Christians view the right to vote as a stewardship issue, knowing that to be a good steward of your voice, you have to research the issues and candidates. The knowledge that accompanies research becomes conviction, and conviction becomes commitment. That's when you say, "This is the most important election ever—I know, because I have done my homework."

RIGHTS AND WRONGS

Twenty years before Jefferson and Adams were political opponents, they were unlikely allies. Jefferson was a Virginian who owned hundreds of slaves in the heart of tobacco country, while Adams was a defense attorney in

Boston. Yet they both understood that the critical issue facing the American colonies concerned the source of human rights. Were those rights rooted in the divine image, granted by God, and thus "unalienable"? Or were they bestowed by a king—who could revoke them at his pleasure?

This question provoked Adams and Jefferson to labor together, persuading others to see that the British monarchy was nothing less than an assault on the divine origin of human rights. They pled with others to join with them, and they literally declared their independence from England with these words: "We hold these truths to be self-evident, that all men are created equal, that they are endowed by their Creator with certain unalienable Rights, that among these are Life, Liberty and the pursuit of Happiness." Jefferson and Adams argued successfully that God entrusted certain rights to every person, and the role of government is not to *bestow* them, but to *ensure* them.

How would you answer the question *Where do our rights come from*? Your answer will likely reveal your perspective of a citizen's responsibility to government and, conversely, of a government's responsibility to each citizen. This perspective will then have a domino effect on other questions, like these:

What does a good citizen look like?

What does a good government look like?

Is a good government one that legislates the office-holders' version of morality and tells people what they should believe?

Or is a good government one that takes a minimalist approach, engaging solely to protect citizens' rights and to administer justice?

These questions get even more complicated when applied to real-world events. If somebody smashes your car window and steals your purse or iPhone, you want the police, FBI, and Homeland Security to dust for fingerprints, interrogate your neighbors, and subpoena video surveillance from every video-recording doorbell within a two-mile radius. In other words, you want government intervention.

On the other hand, if your neighbor four blocks away is burgled, you might think it government overreach to require every neighbor within a two-mile radius to contribute to a taxpayer-funded manhunt for the culprit. Who is right? And what about when the issue isn't burglary but taxes? Health insurance? Vaccination? Education? Welfare? Religious freedom?

Fortunately, the one who designed government has given us principles to help us navigate those issues. The Bible reveals to us the source of unalienable rights as well as the role government should play to protect those rights.

IN THE BEGINNING

The word *genesis* is Greek for "origins," so it is fitting that the book of Genesis describes the creation and implementation of all that is fundamental about human society. Genesis shows the creation of planets and stars, plants and animals, and even human life. We learn where sin came from and how God designed atonement, sacrifices, and the priesthood. Genesis also reveals the origin of marriage, family, food, weather, and nations. Even government is introduced to the world in Genesis. To understand how God designed government to work, it is critical that we understand when and why God introduced it.

It may surprise you, but governments did not originate at Creation. When God rested on the seventh day, there were animals and people, but no government. Even after sin entered the world, government did not. When Cain murdered Abel, God became the legal system and meted out judgment himself (Gen. 4:15). In fact, for the first eight chapters of Genesis, the sparsely populated earth operated without government or nations.

In the absence of earthly authority, sin flourished. Without law enforcement—or even laws—evil proliferated on the earth, making the planet practically unlivable. Moses described it this way:

> Now the earth was corrupt in God's sight, and the earth was filled with *violence*.... And God said to Noah, "I have determined to make an end of all flesh, for the earth is filled with *violence* through them. Behold, I will destroy them with the earth." (Gen. 6:11,13; italics added)

The evil on earth was unparalleled—and what form did that evil take? What was so terrible that God sent a flood to end it? *Violence.*

God responded to the violence by flooding the earth and resetting human society (Gen. 7:22–23). When the flood waters receded, the new beginning came with a new institution—government—to keep the world from regressing to its pre-flood condition. When God established government, he did so to protect human society by shielding it from violence and restraining evil.

The text of this familiar narrative will remind you that the flood waters did not wash away sin. As Noah's family began to repopulate the earth, every human was still born with a sin nature—just like before the flood. Nevertheless, the Lord promised that "never again shall there be a flood to destroy the earth" (Gen. 9:11). God entered into a covenant with Noah's family and provided a mechanism to curb evil and promote human flourishing. The symbol of the covenant is the rainbow. Just as the waters of the flood did not wash away humanity's sin, the rainbow does not restrain it. But it is the sign of God's pledge not to destroy the earth again by deluge and to remind humanity to repent.

Along with the promise symbolized by the rainbow, God set up a new world order, which included a structure of government to restrain the growth of evil. Genesis 9 outlines four blessings for post-flood humanity. As Noah left the ark, God relaunched not only Noah's family but also the entire human race. God sent out Noah's family with a new mandate, similar to what he had given to Adam and Eve (Gen. 1:28–30). This new charge to the post-flood world contained a series of blessings, and protecting these four blessings was to become the main function of human government.

FOUR BLESSINGS

The first post-flood blessing given to mankind was **the freedom to worship.** As Noah and all the ark's inhabitants stepped onto dry ground, Noah's first action was to honor the Lord by building "an altar to Yahweh" (Gen. 8:20a). There, he "took some of every clean animal and some of every clean bird and offered burnt offerings on the altar" (Gen. 8:20b). As far as the text indicates, Noah made this sacrifice not because he was *obligated* but because he was *obliged.* He was thankful. In the post-flood world, Noah had the freedom to worship without the world interfering, corrupting, ridiculing, or rejecting his attempts to worship God in accordance with his conscience.

The Lord perceived the pleasing aroma of Noah's worship and said, "I will never again curse the ground because of man, for the intention of man's heart is evil from his youth. Neither will I ever again strike down every living creature as I have done" (Gen. 8:21). As Noah's family repopulated the earth, this blessing extended to all of their descendants. God allowed people to survive the flood, and that event was commemorated with the freedom to worship.

The second post-flood blessing is **family**. Immediately after receiving Noah's sacrifice, God reiterated mankind's duty to "be fruitful and multiply and fill the earth" (Gen. 9:1b). God did not limit the number of people on the earth; rather, he commanded that the earth be filled with people.

This charge should cause the reader to remember the initial creation mandate (Gen. 1:28–29). God had designed marriage to be a blessing—in fact, he had literally described the charge to be fruitful and multiply as a blessing (Gen. 1:28). This is why a marriage is described in happy and celebratory terms (e.g., Genesis 2:23–25). Children were part of that blessing, and thus, they, too, were designed to bring their family joy.

The blessing of family is one of the highest joys imaginable—so much so that later, Peter would refer to marriage as "the grace of life," and Solomon would declare, "He who finds a wife, finds a good thing" (1 Pet. 3:7; Prov. 18:22). The blessing and joys of family have their roots in this mandate given to Noah: "And God *blessed* Noah and his sons and said to them, 'be fruitful and multiply and fill the earth'" (Gen. 9:1; italics added). The blessing of family had not been washed away with the flood.

The third blessing after the flood is God's provision of **food for humanity**. The pre-flood world obviously had food, yet God reiterated this blessing to Noah, and in so doing, he signaled an important shift. Before the fall, animals and humans lived in a harmonious relationship. Animals came when called and interacted peacefully with people (Gen. 7:8). But after the flood, fear of mankind fell on animals as they became part of the human food chain:

> The fear of you and the dread of you shall be upon every beast of the earth and upon every bird of the heavens, upon everything that creeps on the ground and all the fish of the sea. Into your hand they are delivered. Every moving thing that lives shall be food for you. And as I

gave you the green plants, I give you everything. (Gen. 9:2–3)

After spending more than a year afloat, the animals had plenty of cause to run off the ark.[1] Noah's sacrifices gave them another reason to flee, and they have been fleeing ever since.

You may wonder why God calls the animals' fear of humans a blessing. Well, animals can seriously hurt us! A deer may seem beautiful and tranquil from the safety of your porch, but that same deer would trample you in a fight. He or she is equipped with sharp hooves and— depending on its gender—a rack that could shish-kebab you and make *you* roadkill. Raccoons look cute, but do not try to give one a hug. It is a blessing that, for the most part, the animals that could harm us tend to leave us alone.

But God didn't settle for mere apathy between mankind and the animal world. Better yet, God declared that these animals could be hunted for our food.

God's post-flood world order included blessings such as the **freedom to worship**, a **family to love**, **nature to eat**— and a fourth gift: **life to be protected**. His charge to mankind culminates with this:

> And for your lifeblood I will require a reckoning: from every beast I will require it and from man. From his fellow man I will require a reckoning for the life of man.
>
> Whoever sheds the blood of man, by man shall his blood be shed, for God made man in his own image. (Gen. 9:5–6)

27

This is the genesis of human government. In these verses, God declares life valuable—human life in particular, having "made man in his own image." Before the flood, violence reigned among humans, and God strove against them (Gen. 6:3, 5–6). After the flood, God passed this responsibility to man. From this point forward, society is supposed to be structured to ensure that when violence occurs, justice is administered. God has instituted human government.

A SHORT HISTORY OF VIOLENCE

The pre-flood world and the post-flood world turn on the hinge presented in Genesis 8:20–9:6. Before the flood, people worshiped God by offering sacrifices. Before the flood, people belonged to families. Before the flood, the earth provided food for humans. All these were true after the flood as well, with one addition: God established government to protect mankind from injustice.

By way of comparison, consider Genesis 4:10–12, before the flood. After Cain committed the first murder, God (not government) interrogated and judged him:

> What have you done? The voice of your brother's blood is crying to me from the ground. And now you are cursed from the ground, which has opened its mouth to receive your brother's blood from your hand. When you work the ground, it shall no longer yield to you its strength. You shall be a fugitive and a wanderer on the earth. (Gen. 4:10–12)

That is the punishment Cain received for murdering Abel: he became a fugitive. In other words, he could not farm, own land, or work a field; he would be a nomad and a wanderer. God's punishment struck at Cain's heart, and he lamented:

> My punishment is greater than I can bear. Behold, you have driven me today away from the ground, and from your face I shall be hidden. I shall be a fugitive and a wanderer on the earth, and whoever finds me will kill me. (Gen. 4:13–14)

But God mercifully intervened and protected Cain's life, saying, "Not so! If anyone kills Cain, vengeance shall be taken on him sevenfold" (Gen. 4:15). And off Cain went: "Then Cain went away from the presence of Yahweh and settled in the land of Nod, east of Eden" (Gen. 4:16).

Although the narrative spans only a few verses, Cain's family spans six generations, and by Genesis 4:19, a descendant named Lamech has introduced the world to polygamy and a whole host of other wicked acts, while boasting about them:

> Adah and Zillah, hear my voice, you wives of Lamech, listen to what I say. I have killed a man for wounding me, a young man for striking me. If Cain's revenge is sevenfold, then Lamech's is seventy-sevenfold. (Gen. 4:23–24)

Do you see what Lamech was doing? He was acting with impunity, murdering whomever he wanted, and saying, *"Whatcha gonna do about it? If you thought Cain was untouchable—just look at me!"*

Genesis reveals that from the first murder to the day God closed the ark door, wickedness multiplied. Murder filled the headlines. Killing was commonplace.

So God enacted a change after the flood, establishing government to protect mankind against the violence to which sinful people are prone. After the flood, God sent a message: you cannot murder without other people coming after you. This passage does not use the term *government*, but its genesis is evident. The next chapter (Genesis 10) will introduce nations to the world, and Genesis 11 will introduce languages. But government has its birth in Genesis 9, and it was born for the purpose of keeping violence in check and protecting the blessings of the post-flood world.

FOUR PROTECTIONS OF GOVERNMENT

These four interconnected blessings make life in the post-flood world functional and enjoyable. They require collaboration to function at peak performance. The four blessings become the four functions of government:

1. To protect the freedom to worship

2. To protect family

3. To protect food

4. To protect life

Because government is introduced to the world in this narrative, it is right to read the context to discover what God designed government to do and to be. Since government is tied to these four blessings, it is appropriate to see the preservation of these blessings as precisely what God called government to do.

PROTECTING WORSHIP

Government's first function is to protect the freedom to worship and the freedom to serve God as one's conscience dictates. The First Amendment to the US Constitution does not grant humans the right to worship freely. God does. Worship was the first thing Noah chose to do when his feet touched dry ground. The "freedom of worship" is not some arbitrary American spin that jibes well with a political base. Rather, by God's design, government has the obligation to protect religious freedom.

Let's dive deeper into the government's job to protect freedom to worship. The government must allow and protect the citizens' freedom of conscience to worship God however they see fit. Christians believe freedom to worship—or freedom of religion—transcends what happens on Sunday morning; it touches every area of life, because all of life is lived in worship of God.

By extension, this freedom also applies to people who choose *not* to believe in God, the Bible, or Jesus as their Savior. "Freedom to worship," rightly understood, is not an argument that the government should tell everyone to worship Yahweh. Rather, it means the government should ensure that everyone who desires to worship him *can*. Let's state it clearly: government protects the freedom to worship but does not make worship compulsory.

This is why Baptists have historically advocated for religious freedom for Jews, Muslims, Mormons, and Catholics. If the government prefers or sponsors one belief system over another, persecution of all others is soon to follow.

Did God mess up here by allowing, and even providing protection for, religious freedom? Was God shocked when humanity, a few generations after the flood, used its freedom not to follow him? Of course not. God knew people would go their own way and worship whatever idols and gods they wanted to. That is what Genesis 10 and 11 describes. Remember the Tower of Babel? God used that occasion to multiply and scatter nations throughout the globe. God does not fear religious freedom; he invented it.

The apostle Paul affirmed as much in his gospel sermon on Mars Hill in ancient Athens. Preaching to pagan worshipers he hoped would exercise their freedom to follow Christ, Paul said:

> And he made from one man every nation of mankind to live on all the face of the earth, having determined allotted periods and the boundaries of their dwelling place, that they should seek God, and perhaps feel their way toward him and find him. (Acts 17:26–27)

Paul indicated that God let the nations go their own way so that when they were unable to find peace on their own, they would turn to the one true God. God "hardwired" the desire to worship into the heart of every human being, knowing that scattered people will eventually search for a savior—or some idolatrous alternative.

The freedom to worship points to the plan of God—he created humans with a desire to recognize eternity set in their hearts (Eccles. 3:11). Government's job is to protect the right of people to worship, even though most people who worship do not worship properly. Most do not even worship the one true God. Nonetheless, the government must protect the rights of individuals to search for a savior, so that those who want to respond to God's offer of salvation through Jesus can.

PROTECTING THE FAMILY

After protecting worship, the second obligation of government is to protect the family. God designed the family unit as the foundational building block of society. It is perhaps the most obvious example of the common grace God gives. The family is designed by God to be fruitful and multiply and to glorify God in a myriad of other ways. But high on the list of God's purposes for family is to bring joy to the world (e.g., Exod. 20:12; Ps. 127:3–5; Prov. 17:6).

The blessing of family is arguably the centerpiece of God's new world order. None of the other blessings or commands can exist or be carried out until humans do one thing consistently: make babies and raise them to enjoy the blessings of freedom to worship God, enjoy other people, enjoy food and the fruits of one's labor, and enjoy all these in the relative safety of a just society.

At the most basic level, subduing the earth requires more than eight people. Had Noah not multiplied and begun to fill the earth, there would be no farms, no languages, no government, and no nations. And if there were no nations, then there would be no great commission, no global evangelization, and no concept of a gospel that transcends ethnic and linguistic distinctions. Without the family, there would not be a "world" for Jesus to save (1 John 4:14).

Even Jesus, the Son of God born as a human, was born into a family. The concept of family is so basic—it is the very fabric of God's design for society.

Naturally, family precedes government. When the world attempts to exploit children, the family unit is the first line of defense. Government is to cooperate with parents for the protection of the family and of children.

Perhaps this is why the concept of family is often under attack. When people want to lash out at God, they do so by attacking that which he designed. They seek to devalue marriage, gender, and parenting. Marriage is seen as optional, gender as arbitrary, and children as an obstacle to success. While an examination of any of those three issues is outside the scope of this book, it is critical to understand that God made government with the goal of protecting the blessings of family. A government that redefines marriage, promotes gender ambiguity, or tolerates abortion has ceased to function properly and has failed at one of its most basic tasks.

PROTECTING THE FOOD SUPPLY

The third function of government is admittedly less controversial than the others: to protect natural resources, and the food supply in particular. This is a subset of the broader creation mandate from Genesis 2:15: "Yahweh took man and put him in the garden of Eden to work it and keep it." *Protecting* is a good translation of the Hebrew word the ESV renders *keep* in Genesis 2. For mankind to be good stewards of the earth requires our preservation and protection of various potentials for beauty and utility.

But after the flood, God zeroes in on the food supply in Genesis 9:3 when he repeats the creation mandate. He says: "Every moving thing that lives shall be food for you. And as I gave you the green plants, I give you everything."

Thus, in the establishment of government, God specifically points to the protection of the food supply as one of the government's main functions. It is simple to see why this is so significant. We don't want salmonella in our lettuce, and we like the idea of someone in authority saying, "No, you can't earn money by feeding people this contaminated food." We want inspectors to give their seal of approval and protect us from botulism and rancid meat. God gave humans plants and animals to eat as part of his new world order, and the government has an obligation to guard the food supply chain.

This obligation is bigger than merely food. Certainly, it extends to the seas and water as well (Gen. 9:2). A lost hiker can live for weeks without food but only a matter of days without water. Food would not do someone any good if they lived in Chernobyl, where the water is poisoned. This is why God commands mankind to protect the natural resources of the land and sea. It is not for the limited purposes of biodiversity—as noble as they may be—

but rather for creating the conditions for human thriving (cf. Gen 1:26, 28).

But, as we often do, our era of government has put the cart before the horse. Too many times, the government overreaches, placing an undue burden on farmers and taking too much responsibility (freedom) away from consumers. For example, fruit producers may face watering restrictions because an endangered owl needs a different kind of hydrated habitat, or the water that could be used for farms is flushed into the ocean to protect smelt.[2] Some forms of environmentalism can shift the balance of power, twisting the purpose of government to favor an owl's nest over a human's need for produce.

I'm not advocating for the destruction of an endangered species; God calls us to be good stewards of nature (Gen. 1:29–30, 2:15, 9:3; Ps. 24:1; Prov. 12:10, 27:18). In fact, the duty to steward creation is wrapped up in the original mandate given to Adam and Eve (Gen. 1:26). When Moses summarized the charge God gave mankind, he said it was to both "work" and "keep" the garden (Gen. 2:15). But the blessing described in Genesis 9 does not call us to prioritize animals at any cost. The blessing (and therefore, the government's obligation) is to protect our ability to have ample food and safe water.

A strong government ensures the safety and availability of food in a way that is compatible with the protection of the beauty of God's creation. It should ensure a balance between both "working" and "keeping" the land. God has not called governments to regulate ocean levels but to regulate the food supply from both ocean and land.

There must be a responsible form of environmentalism that preserves flora and fauna in a manner consistent with human flourishing. The health of humanity literally depends on it.

PROTECTING LIFE

The blessings of worship, family, and the abundance that God has set before humanity for its enjoyment rest on a premise: humans have to be alive and free to enjoy those blessings.

Therefore, God's fourth obligation for government towers above all others. God told Noah, "Whoever sheds the blood of man, by man shall his blood be shed, for God made man in his own image" (Gen. 9:6). This is the all-important verse in which God establishes government—but this time, note the conjunction *for.* Why should men enforce justice and redouble violence against the violent? *Because God made man in his own image.*

The animals do not have this distinction. The family does not either—even though the Godhead includes the Father and the Son. Food is not packaged with a label stating "Made in the image of God." The only thing said to be in the image of God is every individual man, woman, and child. We have the ability to worship God, to reflect his attributes, and to magnify the glory of God by how we live, serve, and worship.

Animals are fruitful and multiply because they are put on the earth to serve the needs of humanity. Humans are fruitful and multiply because we magnify the image of

God. Humans should not kill an animal out of sheer cruelty or for an immoral reason, but when they do, the offense does not approach the severity of killing another human. God established government because attacks on human life were growing more frequent from the days of Cain to the days of Noah.

It is impossible to overstate how important this obligation of government is. Protecting human life is foundational to all other obligations. If government officials allow cracks to exist in this foundational obligation, it little matters how effective they are at the others—and they are likely to let those crack as well.

UNALIENABLE RIGHTS COME FROM GOD

Let's fast forward several thousand years—to the present. If you're reading this, you're most likely an American living several millennia after God instituted government—in a republic less than a quarter millennium old. Other than the Bible, the most significant documents informing your worldview of government are the Declaration of Independence and the US Constitution.

Maybe you know all three of these sources well. Maybe you know just one well. It may be that some people don't know either of America's founding documents, let alone the Bible, well enough to be reasonably and passionately convinced that *the rights affirmed in all three documents come from God and cannot rightfully be taken from people by any ruler but God.*

Again, this is not American Christian spin; you have seen it yourself in Genesis 1–9. Some of us have forgotten the truth—or have feared to affirm the truth—buried in the second paragraph of the Declaration of Independence: "We hold these truths to be self-evident, that all men are created equal, that they are endowed by their Creator with certain unalienable Rights, that among these are Life, Liberty and the pursuit of Happiness." Both Genesis and the Declaration affirm that our rights "are endowed by" our Creator—not by the government.

Why is this so important? When you believe it is the government that bestows your rights, you look to the government instead of to God as having the final say about the purpose and parameters of your existence. You trust in the government for protection, provision, and prosperity. You look to the government for your paycheck, health care, and education. The government becomes the warehouse of your rights, and government programs become the pipeline of your wealth and identity. And if you believe that, you'll be using your life to advocate for all kinds of solutions God did not design government to be capable of producing.

GOING ROGUE

Naturally, people who don't know or don't believe that government's purpose and boundaries are defined by Scripture use government to advance whatever seems good to them—no holds barred.

Sadly, even many Christians have disregarded God's boundaries for government and set up their own boundaries (or none at all). Don't get me wrong: the idea of molding society into whatever image my community of likeminded thinkers wants—or thinks God wants—sounds tempting. But that's not why God instituted government or how he designed government, so it doesn't work that way, no matter how hard people try to force it.

When churches view the government as an agent for moral advancement, they transfer to the government their obligation to proclaim morality and to practice righteousness. The church—the group that God ordained to be the moral voice of society—deputizes a secular government to be the agent of morality. This partnership may sound appealing on the surface, but this level of cooperation between the church and government inevitably leads to compromise—and not the good kind. This kind of political activism in a church corrupts the church. Churches that look to the government to advance a political agenda will drift into liberal theology. Compromise compels doctrinal drift.

REPAIRING THE FOUNDATION

Genesis 9 is just one of many Scripture passages that allow us to state with confidence that the Bible rebukes a government that allows citizens to be enslaved, discriminated against, starved, and robbed, and to have their families encroached on. God will hold accountable the men and women behind an unjust government.

But the existence of bad leaders does not imply the original design was flawed. Genesis 9 displays God's plan for government to *protect* freedoms, not to *provide* them. To use a sports metaphor, God designed government to play defense, not offense. It exists to protect field position, not to acquire it.

People have "unalienable rights" because they are made in the image of God, and God designed government to protect these rights that he himself extended. This doesn't preclude people from banding together to advance agendas that benefit society. But this activity is a function of common grace—as people seek to right wrongs and live out their love for their neighbors. That kind of social action is a response to injustice—such as lobbying to end tax-payer-funded abortion or to oppose the immoral actions of wicked foreign governments which are harming their people. That sort of social action has been a hallmark of Christian ethics and is a response to sin in the world. It is categorically distinct from looking to government to advance a social agenda.

The simplest way to put it is this: God bestows unalienable rights, and he charges government with one task: *protect them.* A government that fails to protect becomes a fountain of harm.

Back in 2016, *Psychology Today* published an article by David Niose entitled "The Danger of Claiming Our Rights Come from God." Though he argues from different footing, he is exploring the same position we are: *Do rights originate with God or with the government?*

He throws a bone to those of us who believe in God-given rights before he bares his teeth and tries to shred the biblical position:

It's nice to have a philosophical basis for the view that government can't deny our God-given rights. Unfortunately, however, the entire argument falls apart under scrutiny, and in fact, it can more accurately be understood as a disingenuous attempt to promote religion while doing nothing to explain or secure anyone's rights.

First, let's consider the claim that "our rights come from God." Since even believers will acknowledge that the very existence of God cannot be proven, this claim leaves us in a most unsettling position: Our most precious rights are apparently flowing from an entity whose existence can reasonably be doubted. Even believers acknowledge that faith, as opposed to verifiable evidence, is the basis of their belief. That's fine for one's personal religious outlook, but why would we feel that cherished human rights and civil rights are more secure if they arise from a source that may not even exist?[3]

Obviously Niose was wrong when he wrote "even believers will acknowledge that the very existence of God cannot be proven." But never mind that. His larger point is worth understanding: for human rights to be secure, the source of those rights must be secure. For Niose, who doubts the existence of God, a Christian belief in rights coming from God seems to lack security. But evaluating a secular view of government with this lens proves it is a defenseless perspective. If you believe it is the government's job to procure and advance rights, then your rights are only as secure as your government is. If the government has failed to grant rights, you're out of luck, with no rational or spiritual basis to object that you're being mistreated.

It is far more logically consistent and practically defensible to hold the biblical view of government: God blessed humanity with the rights to worship freely, to build families, to have food, and to live. And he established government to protect these rights, for our good and for his glory—that we may worship him freely and enjoy life's blessings.

But governments, like people, fall short. When the ship is headed in the wrong direction, it's not because ships are a bad means of traversing water. It's because sinful people are steering the ship. And when the ship *is* sailing in the wrong direction—should we obey it?

---

[1] Comparing the dates of Genesis 7:11 with Genesis 8:11–14 reveals the animals (and people) had been on the ark for just over a year.

[2] See Erik Telford, "California wasting water due to fish and inefficiency," *The San Diego Union-Tribune*, December 2, 2015, https://www.sandiegouniontribune.com/opinion/commentary/sdut-california-water-drought-2015dec02-story.html; Jane Kay, "Delta Smelt, Icon of California Water Wars, Is Almost Extinct," *National Geographic*, April 3, 2015, https://www.nationalgeographic.com/science/article/150403-smelt-california-bay-delta-extinction-endangered-species-drought-fish.

[3] David Niose, "The Danger of Claiming That Rights Come from God," *Psychology Today*, Sussex Publishers, October 6, 2016, www.psychologytoday.com/us/blog/our-humanity-naturally/201610/the-danger-claiming-rights-come-god.

2

HOW CHRISTIANS SHOULD RELATE TO GOVERNMENT

An unconstitutional law or commandment is a nullity;
no man sins in disregarding it. He disobeys, however, at
his peril.

— Charles Hodge

It may seem farfetched, but some environmental
activists believe that white vehicles would help reverse
global warming. Google it and you can read the argument.
After all, white cars reflect heat while darker hues absorb
it, requiring more time with the AC on. More AC results in
increased carbon output, thereby contributing to global
warming.[1] Other environmentalists argue the opposite:
that white car roofs would make the atmosphere warmer.[2]
Either way, a mass installation of white roofs could have
unintended consequences, such as leading to reduced rain-
fall in some regions.[3]

Let's imagine for a moment that, on the whole, environmentalists grant the net gains of requiring everyone to drive cars with white roofs would be negligible, but that the sacrifice would be worth it because it would demonstrate that Americans are taking global warming seriously. Imagine that activists started lobbying Congress for a law that mandates that everybody drive white vehicles.

Kowtowed to by the environmentalist lobby, congressional leaders rush the bill through. It cruises through the House and then the Senate with a filibuster-proof majority, fueled further by automotive lobbyists who would benefit from increased car sales, and the president signs the bill into law.

You wake up one morning only to discover that you are now required by federal law to drive a white vehicle. No problem. Your truck is white. But your wife and her navy-blue minivan are in violation. The fork in the road is complicated: to ignore the white vehicle federal mandate is to disobey the government, and disobedience to the authorities is a sin. Is God telling her to schedule a paint job in order to submit to the authority God has instituted?

This chapter will address this question. We have been taught (and have taught others) that Christians are to obey the government in all things, unless the government commands us to sin. I will argue that the often-used maxim *Obey always, unless sin is commanded* does not present what the Bible actually teaches and models concerning how Christians are to relate to government. To that end:

- I will flesh out **two imperatives** we must observe in Romans 13, including God's purposes for them and how they bless people.
- I will sketch out **three motivations** Christians have for obeying the imperatives.
- I will map out **four limitations** of the imperatives—i.e., where our obligations to obey cease.

IS THE GOVERNMENT GOD?

The truth is that the conventional wisdom which says *Obey the government at all times unless it calls you to sin* is woefully inadequate and gives government a level of deference that is owed only to God. So where did that concept come from, and how did it become entrenched in evangelical thinking?

Prior to the Protestant Reformation, the Catholic Church was the law throughout Europe. It approved the Holy Roman emperor and expected all government officials to be under church authority. The idea that the government could command you to sin was a logical nullity: to obey the government was to obey the Church, and the Church was led by the pope; therefore, the law of the land was the law of the Lord.

An excommunicated Martin Luther wrestled with how to instruct Christians to relate to government. He, and the first generation of Lutherans along with him, provided a limiting principle which eventually became enshrined in the Augsburg Confession: obedience is owed to the government and magistrates at all times, "save only

47

when they command sin."[4] This was huge, because it represented a divergence from Catholicism. It allowed for occasions of disobedience. This is the view that is common in American churches today.

But did it go far enough? Some other early Protestants who had broken away from both the pope and the Holy Roman emperor (people like John Calvin and the English and Scottish Puritans) saw that the Lutheran view of government was too expansive. By teaching that government is owed allegiance at all times—except in rare cases of commanding sin—the Lutherans ended up demanding an allegiance to government that exclusively belongs to God. It is no wonder this Lutheran view is the one often held by those who see the church and state as being in partnership to advance the kingdom of God on earth.

Thus, many English-speaking Protestants (along with Calvin) charted a different course. Puritans taught that the king was himself a subject of God, and his ability to administer laws was limited by God's word. For this reason, the Westminster Assembly declared that government was designed by God to *check evil* and to *promote good*. Any laws inside of those parameters were "lawful," and Christians were to submit only to "lawful commands."[5] By insisting on the word "lawful," the Puritans were creating distance between themselves and government and were defining a more nuanced ethic than that of the Lutherans. They were permitting a looser standard for obedience but not requiring it. This wiggle room allowed them to discern the *what* and the *why* behind government commands—and whether they were bound to obey. After all, the government is not God, but the government is established by God to further his purposes on earth.

This is exactly the ethic we see taught in the New Testament's longest passage concerning government, Romans 13:1–7:

> Let every person be subject to the governing authorities. For there is no authority except from God, and those that exist have been instituted by God. Therefore whoever resists the authorities resists what God has appointed, and those who resist will incur judgment. For rulers are not a terror to good conduct, but to bad. Would you have no fear of the one who is in authority? Then do what is good, and you will receive his approval, for he is God's servant for your good. But if you do wrong, be afraid, for he does not bear the sword in vain. For he is the servant of God, an avenger who carries out God's wrath on the wrongdoer. Therefore one must be in subjection, not only to avoid God's wrath but also for the sake of conscience. For because of this you also pay taxes, for the authorities are ministers of God, attending to this very thing. Pay to all what is owed to them: taxes to whom taxes are owed, revenue to whom revenue is owed, respect to whom respect is owed, honor to whom honor is owed.

UNDERSTANDING THE IMPERATIVES

Paul issued two imperatives in Romans 13:1–7. He began by commanding Christians to be subject to the authorities, and he ended by demanding they pay their taxes.

Note that the command to "be subject to the governing authorities" is immediately tied to the reality that their authority is derived from God's design for government: "for there is no authority except from God." Understanding God's basic design for government is therefore key to interpreting the imperatives of Romans 13.

DESIGN CHECK

Do you remember in the previous chapter how we covered the sinfulness of the world before the flood? Violence had grown out of control, to the point that God flooded the world to stop it. Government was God's design to keep that from happening again.

God designed the government *to punish evil* and *to promote good*. Paul writes, "Therefore whoever resists the authorities resists what God has appointed, and those who resist will incur judgment. For rulers are not a terror to good conduct, but to bad" (Rom. 13:2–3a). In other words, God designed government to terrorize bad conduct. But if you obey authority, you might get a reward: "Would you have no fear of the one who is in authority? Then do what is good, and you will receive his approval" (Rom. 13:3b). If you do bad, you get the sword. If you do good, you get a reward. This is because government is God's servant to execute wrath, and government is God's servant for your good. Government serves God by giving good to good people. Government also serves God by giving evil to evil people. This is how God designed the world to work.

This principle is true on both a personal and national level. On the personal level, consider again Lamech (from Genesis 4). Had he existed after the flood, when he said, "Today, I feel like I'm going to kill one person or seven people or seventy-seven people," he (in theory) would have been killed by his government before he crossed that line. That is the effect of checking evil.

What works at the personal level is scalable at the national level, too. God designed governments to constrain each other.

At the Tower of Babel (in Genesis 11), people were collaborating and conspiring to use government for evil. They said, "Come, let us build ourselves a city and a tower with its top in the heavens, and let us make a name for ourselves, lest we be dispersed over the face of the whole earth" (Gen. 11:4). Their attempt to build a tower showed their distrust in God and their disdain for his command for mankind to spread out on the earth (Gen. 9:1). Perhaps their motivation in building a tower was to escape a future flood, or perhaps it was an expression of their desire to get to heaven in order to be like God. Either way, it was sinful, and God brought their enterprise to a dramatic end, toppling the tower and casting out its occupants. He confused their language and designed things so that from that point forward, nation would check nation. The people's plans to operate a one-world government dissolved by necessity, and many smaller clans and governments sprang up. Just as one man can't become particularly evil before the government intervenes, now one nation can't become particularly evil before other nations intervene.

This is why Paul can describe wicked governments as fulfilling God's plan for the world. His point is that even pagan governments check evil. This restraint is what makes the world livable. One country cannot grow in unbridled evil without being reined in by others. As Rome grew larger, other nations rose up against it. When Napoleon tried to conquer Mexico, he was stopped. As England strove to expand its empire and dominate the world, colonial governments rebelled in North America and India. This is God's way to check evil. Countries punish evildoers inside their borders, and they punish each other outside of them.

This is true regardless of a nation's motives. When Alexander the Great went to war against the Persian Empire, it didn't matter which empire was more righteous or who had more justification for territorial claims around the Mediterranean. Countries check each other, and that keeps evil in check.

Even wicked governments sometimes suppress evil effectively. It's been said that life for Christians in Saddam Hussein's Iraq was significantly better than life under ISIS or its current form of government. One wicked regime may keep an alternative wicked regime from rising to power, and that is just the way the world functions.

The same can be true of relatively upright regimes. In his book *The Four Loves*, C. S. Lewis describes a reality that is hard for many Americans to understand. He says you can have two different people on two different sides of a war, and both are operating in righteousness—both are fighting to suppress evil. They might even pause the battle and have a Bible study together.

Similarly, at the local level, you can have Christian prosecutors and public defenders who are trying the same case, and neither one is sinning. In a local government, innocent people can be accused of crimes, and police can make mistakes, but the government still bears a sword to bring peace.

This is the basic way God designed the world and government to work after the flood. Importantly, it is the government's job to punish evil—which means it is not *your* job to do so (unless that is literally what the government pays you to do). In Romans 13:4, Paul says the civil authorities can be an avenger, as they are the ones who bear the sword. That word *avenge* is a Septuagint word—the Greek translation of the Old Testament—for *the avenger of blood.* Under Moses's Law, if you accidentally killed someone in an act of manslaughter (not murder), a family member of your victim was allowed to appoint an avenger of blood who could go after you to pursue justice. However, you could run to another city to seek refuge (Num. 35).

By the time Paul wrote to the Roman Christians, government had long become the avenger bearing the sword. It was and is government's job to track the murderer down. If somebody robs you, you don't have to become a vigilante, because your local police department will respond. If somebody assaults you, it is the government's job to take care of it. They are the professionals. They are the avengers toward evildoers.

Even a wicked government can check evil and pro-mote peace; even wicked governments have been estab-lished by God for that purpose. Paul recognizes that every government has this ability when he writes that "those [governments] that exist have been instituted by God." In fact, even wicked governments derive their mandate to rule from God's design for government found in Genesis 8–9. So, when a wicked government makes lawful demands on its citizens, Christians are called to obey. By "lawful," I mean commands that promote peace or hinder evil.

If we are to obey only lawful commands (i.e., con-sistent with God's ordained purpose for government to check evil and promote good), then what does it mean to be submissive to ungodly leaders? This is an important question, because there is no place on earth where either a society or the government fully embraces biblical princi-ples. No nation has only the Bible as the law of the land. In fact, government leaders often reject the Bible—and yet we are called to be subject to them. So any (and *every!*) application of Romans 13:1–7 is going to take place in the context of ungodly leadership—including the context in which Paul wrote Romans.

Imagine the least democratic form of government you can. Conjure up a vision of a totalitarian leader who wields absolute power. Give him a massive army with which to terrorize his subjects and expand his empire. He attacks neighboring nations and enslaves those who op-pose his aggression, resettling them in a different part of the world. He's so brutal and monstrous that he tortures

Christians, feeding them to lions and burning them alive for his entertainment.

Such a description is not hypothetical; this was the world in which Paul lived under the emperor Nero. Nero was a brutal dictator who fed Christians to lions and turned believers into torches for his own sadistic pleasure.

Nero reigned when Paul wrote to the Christians in Rome. This reality did not stop Paul from writing "Let every person be subject to the governing authorities.... Therefore one must be in subjection.... Pay to all what is owed to them" (Rom. 13:1, 5, 7). Paul even wrote that the civil authority is "God's servant for your good," and that he is "the servant of God" (Rom. 13:4).

This was not written by Jonathan Edwards regarding the British king. This was not written by George Washington, Thomas Jefferson, or John Adams regarding themselves. This was written by the apostle Paul to people who were suffering under a maliciously unrighteous ruler. Christians would have been tempted to apostatize because of the persecution they were facing. Initially, when Christianity began to spread, they were protected. Jews had a certain amount of limited protection, but roughly ten years after the book of Romans was written, that would change.

During this time, if believers claimed they were Jews, Rome would protect them, but the Jews would have persecuted them. If they proclaimed allegiance to King Jesus, they were subject to beatings and martyrdom by both Rome and the Jews. Paul himself was seized and beaten by Jewish leaders before being handed over to Rome. He was beaten as a Roman citizen, put on trial before governors (and Caesar), and eventually martyred.

It is while walking a fatal path that Paul tells believers to be subject to the authorities and to pay what is owed, be it money, respect, or honor. He tells them not only to be subject to them but also to honor their king and governing authorities.

Why would God command believers to respect, honor, and submit to such an abusive authority? If, as the Westminster Confession states, we are to obey only "lawful" laws, how can anything commanded by ungodly leadership be lawful?

The commands of ungodly leaders are lawful insofar as they check evil and promote good. An otherwise heinous civil authority who issues a lawful command is to be obeyed in that instance, for he is acting within the specific reason God instituted government. This is the kernel of Paul's imperatives.

Simply put, God uses ungodly leaders to check evil and promote good. Certainly not everything an evil ruler does is lawful, because not everything he does would check evil or promote good. But that which is lawful should be obeyed, even when it is a "Nero" who commands it.

The truth is, ungodly governments can protect freedoms, create a stable culture for the flourishing of family, ensure food, and protect life. This is a particularly important truth for American Christians to understand: the Bible does command obedience, even to wicked leaders, when they are acting within the limited sphere for which God instituted government.

Does it seem like a stretch to say that even Nero's ungodly government created a stable culture and protected life? The Roman Empire had indeed brought stability to a large swath of the world's population. It ushered in a stable economy, a nearly global network of roads and currency, as well as arts and culture. I'm not arguing that only governments that promote arts and culture are to be obeyed, but I'm merely making the point that even ungodly governments can be used for the good of society.

Romans 13 is true regardless of whether the emperor is Nero or Constantine. Paul is instructing Christians on how to relate to government, reminding the Romans that government was designed by God. This is not necessarily new revelation Paul is recording, but confirmation and explication of prior revelation (revelation we will look at in more detail in the next chapter). Our task as contemporary readers is not to interpret Romans 13 in light of Nero (or Biden or any other ruler), but rather to interpret Nero (and Biden and every other ruler) in light of Romans 13. Civil leaders are not owed obedience when their commands exceed the limits God has placed on them.

This is good, because no fallen, human authority is going to be a perfect representation of God's morality. In the context of democracy, people say they can't vote for this or that candidate because he or she falls short of biblical ethics in some area. But on this side of God's eternal kingdom, no candidate in any country will perfectly reflect biblical ethics. We live in a fallen world. Our handbook for

Kingdom ethics is the Bible, yet no society on earth has ever lived up to God's design for government. Paul knew this firsthand, yet his command is clear: we are to respect and honor the civil authorities operating within God's design for government, and this is what Romans 13 is all about. We weren't made for this world. But while we're here as strangers, pilgrims, aliens, and exiles, we can respect the government God has instituted as our authority.

SUBJECT TO WHOM?

Paul clarifies the scope of this submission by using a limiting phrase: *governing authorities.* Christians are not called to be subject to all governments in the world. They are not called to be subject to the authorities in countries of which they are not citizens or residents. If an American visits Canada, he is subject to the Canadian authorities for the duration of his visit. But that doesn't mean he is subject to Canadian authorities once he returns home to the US. The governing authorities are those who provide your militia, those who punish wrongdoers, and those who collect your taxes (Rom. 13:2, 4, 6).

It's also important to look at the way nations claim authority over other nations—legitimately and illegitimately. When Iraqi forces invaded Kuwait during the Gulf War in the 1990s, they immediately published new maps that showed Kuwait as a province of Iraq. But finding yourself on a map under a country's jurisdiction doesn't make you a citizen of that country. In Colonial Williamsburg's DeWitt Wallace Museum there is a map on display of the original thirteen colonies of the United States. It's the sort of map George Washington would have had in his pocket as he was surveying the western frontier of Virginia, attempting to evict the French from the Ohio River Valley. The map took the borders of the colonies and simply extended them to the edge of the known world.

Imagine Washington going to the French and the Indians and showing them that map. If you were French—or even an Indian, for that matter—would that map have made a compelling argument for why England should possess the Ohio River? "Look, I've got a map, and it goes on forever." Simply because your location is printed on a map does not make you subject to the authority in that location. The authorities you are subject to are the ones to whom you pay your taxes, who will arrest you if you *don't* pay them, and who punish wrongdoers. You're a citizen of and subject to *that* authority.

Paul is not saying Christians may choose which authorities they prefer. He is saying there is going to be an authority that possesses the right to tax you and to punish you if you don't pay. God has dispatched them for that purpose. Because they can punish, you must pay everything that is owed to them: Taxes to whom taxes are owed, revenue to whom revenue is owed. Good Christians will be good citizens who pay their taxes.

Which leads to a practical observation: most of the time that believers are called to be subject to authority, it is not a king across the ocean or a ruler in the nation's capital that is in mind. It is much more likely that our obedience is going to be seen in the context of local laws, enforced by local law enforcement. We are more likely to have run-ins with the sheriff than with the army, and with the city council than with Congress.

MOTIVATION FOR THE IMPERATIVES

The key to understanding how Christians are to relate to government is to comprehend *why* Paul commands us to be subject to authority and pay our taxes. He gives three distinct motivations: providential, prudential, and personal. If we are to recover the concept of obeying "lawful" commands, we need to grasp the three-motivation progression in Romans 13:1–7.

MOTIVATION #1: PROVIDENTIAL

One motivation for submitting to civil authority is that this also submits to God's providence. Paul says in verse one, "For there is no authority except from God, and those that exist have been instituted by God." This speaks to God's absolute sovereignty over human affairs. He rules the world through his providence, and everything happens under his authority. Every enthroned king, every emperor who reigns over an empire, every governor who occupies the governor's mansion, every mayor, every police officer, every sanitation worker, all the way across the spectrum from municipal to federal government—they are installed by God's providence.

This is true for every person in every walk of life. You have your occupation by the providence of God. He provided the opportunity for you to have your job. You got hired by his will. He is the one who created a world and told you to work in it. His providence directs all of this, and government workers are no different. Whether or not you work for the government, you are working under God's sovereignty and providence.

There is no authority, Paul says, except from God. He designed the existing categories of authority. God alone is the ultimate authority, but God chose to mediate some of his authority in the world through a few authority structures.

In the family, the husband is the head authority figure in the household, and parents have authority over their children. God designed the family to demonstrate such authority (Eph. 5:22–33). Provision and protection are natural benefits to this design (Eph. 6:1–4). These are two examples of God-designed authority.

Your boss is your God-instituted authority at work. A common experience in life is that there is always somebody else in charge. This is by God's providence so that you respect these people. As Paul writes, "Bondservants, obey your earthly masters with fear and trembling, with a sincere heart, as you would Christ" (Eph. 6:5).

Government is another category of authority designed by God. He invented and instituted it to be an authority for restraining evil, which allows humans to flourish—to procreate, worship, learn, own and steward property, innovate, serve one another, and do everything else humans do that reflects the character of their Creator.

The family structure protects children, and the government protects the family structure, ensuring the just sequence of passing down property and wealth. All of this is in God's providential design to protect people and society. That's what government was designed to do (Gen. 9:6; Rom. 13:4).

The teaching that we are to obey authority functioning within God's design does not negate the reality that ungodly leaders exist. We live in a world where authority is abused. For example, when government turns its sword against believers, that becomes persecution. Remember that Paul is writing Romans 13 to people being persecuted by their government, yet God did not institute government to persecute believers. Abuses of authority are sin, and sin does not originate from a holy God. However, just because an authority wrongly uses its power in some instances does not imply a free pass to disobey when that same government uses its authority to create and enforce legitimate laws, by God's providence. Just because one nation is persecuting believers doesn't mean all nations have surrendered their God-ordained authority. God established governments to bear the sword and check evil, even though some nations have sinfully abused that design.

This principle applies to other authority structures as well. For example, some say a husband can't be an authority figure in the home, because there are abusive husbands, and therefore that kind of authority is not from God. An abusive husband is a serious, sinful twisting of God's authority—one that clearly does not come from the hand of a holy God. Nevertheless, God providentially instituted the authority structure of the family with the husband as the leader. When acting within the bounds of God's design for marriage (which include hefty husbandly duties summed up by the charge to love and provide for one's wife as Christ does the church), the husband is authoritative.

To the extent the governing authorities, by God's providence, fulfill their obligations as God designed them, they are "God's servant for your good" (Rom. 13:4). These words would have surprised Paul's readers. The word Paul uses for *servant* is the Greek word *diakonos*, from which we get our word *deacon*. Paul is saying that government workers are God's deacons. They're serving him by serving their country, since a government's function should be to make life better, to be an expression of common grace, to be a steward of financial resources (taxes) and natural resources (the food supply in particular), and to be a protector of the family and of all human life.

Every person who works for the government in that sense is recognized as a deacon by God. Whether they work in the sanitation department or for a public utility's customer service hotline, as a law enforcement officer, a tax collector, or an IRS auditor, each is God's deacon. They're working for the Lord, whether they know him or not.

This holds true regardless of a country's righteousness. In Romans 13, God is calling Nero his servant, his deacon. There's nothing that's *not* offensive in that verse. The God's-servant part would have offended Nero; the Jews would have been offended by Paul's saying God appointed Nero to the throne. But that's the reality of this passage. Providentially, all authority in the world comes from God, including government authority.

MOTIVATION #2: PRUDENTIAL

Sometimes the government steps outside of God's appointed boundaries. Sometimes the government commands things that fall outside of Genesis 9—things that are neither for your good nor done to punish evildoers. What then?

Obviously, God never calls believers to sin, so when a law calls a believer to commit a sinful act, it is to be disobeyed.

But what about a law that might be "morally neutral" yet clearly beyond the scope of what God has installed the government to do? Remember the earlier example of a law that commands everyone to operate white vehicles? Clearly, that law is not "lawful" in that it does not check evil, nor does it promote good. The providential reason to obey the imperatives of Romans 13 does not apply here. It is outside of God's design for government, and thus, even though it comes from a government God has providentially allowed, it is not an expression of God's authority, nor is it a law that has been appointed by God. In fact, it is expressly *outside* of his design for government, and thus, believers are not morally obligated to obey it.

But you still might want to pause before going and buying that red sports car or having your wife dodge around town in the navy-blue minivan. Why? Because otherwise she could be thrown in jail. Or, in other words, because of prudence (practical wisdom).

This is what Paul gets to next in Romans 13. The second motivation you have to obey the government is that you can be punished if you do not. In Romans 13:3–4, Paul says you will be approved by the government if you follow its laws, but you will be punished by the government if you disobey those laws. That's Paul's point here—that government is established by God, and even if the government goes beyond the boundaries that God gave it, you should still probably obey it, because otherwise you will suffer punitive action. If you don't want to do the time, don't do the crime.

This is why the idea of peaceful protesting has always been a staple of Christian civic interaction. Unjust laws exist and can be resisted—but how? When individual Christians resist the law, they resist not by fighting or running from the police. Individual Christians should peacefully resist an unjust or immoral law—and willingly suffer the consequences for their disobedience. This is a basic component of Christian civil disobedience: *sometimes you do disregard the law.* And when you disobey, you fully accept the consequences.[6]

MOTIVATION #3: PERSONAL (CONSCIENCE)

Paul gives a third reason why you might want to obey the government: a moral reason, for the sake of your conscience. It's against Scripture for believers to go against what their conscience says (Acts 23:1; 1 Cor. 8:7–12; 2 Cor. 1:12; 1 Tim 1:5, 19; Heb. 13:18; 1 Pet. 3:16). When your conscience convicts you of sin, listen to it. The conscience is a guide given to all people. That's why Paul could write that non-Jews, who did not receive the Ten Commandments or other parts of the Law from God, "show that the work of the law is written on their hearts, while their conscience also bears witness, and their conflicting thoughts accuse or even excuse them" (Rom. 2:15).

The conscience is a gift to restrain evil, but that doesn't mean the conscience is infallible. Some people's consciences are dulled by repeated sin (Rom. 1:17–32). Other times your conscience might convict you of things that are not sin. For example, in 1 Corinthians 8, Paul explains there is nothing inherently wrong with eating meat offered to idols, because the idols don't actually taint the meat. You can eat the meat with a clear conscience. However, if your conscience bothers you about it, don't eat it, because for you it would be a sin.

In Paul's (and God's) estimation, if your conscience convicts you, it is better for you to refrain from doing something you could lawfully do, because it's better for you to train yourself to listen to your conscience than it is for you to train yourself to go against your conscience. However, you also need to know that your conscience is sometimes wrong, and the solution to that situation is to teach your conscience, not to ignore it. You "grow" your conscience by feeding it the word of God. If your conscience convicts you, then do not eat the meat offered to idols until you have grown more mature in your faith and you can do so with a clear conscience.

Paul is using the same logic here in Romans 13:5: "Therefore one must be in subjection, not only to avoid God's wrath but also for the sake of conscience." So, your wife is going to roll out in her illegal minivan and say, "I'm going to do the time. If they stop me, they can have my

Nissan Quest when they pry it from my cold, dead fingers." But Paul wonders if maybe her conscience will convict her. Your wife may start to feel guilty while she's driving. If so, she should start shopping for a white upgrade.

THE BLESSING OF OBEDIENCE

Thank God for government. Think about it: the world hates the church and will come after us, and in most cases, the government will afford us more protection than we could provide for ourselves. After all, Christians are not to live vengefully but harmoniously:

> Repay no one evil for evil, but give thought to do what is honorable in the sight of all. If possible, so far as it depends on you, live peaceably with all. Beloved, never avenge yourselves, but leave it to the wrath of God, for it is written, "Vengeance is mine, I will repay, says the Lord." To the contrary, "if your enemy is hungry, feed him; if he is thirsty, give him something to drink; for by doing so you will heap burning coals on his head." (Rom. 12:17–20)

If you're living the Romans 12 ethic, you're going to need the Romans 13 protection. If you're in the world turning the other cheek to those who wrong you, there needs to be a government that doesn't turn the other cheek. Jesus said if someone steals your jacket, give him your coat (Matt. 5:40). If she steals one bike, give her your other bike, too. If we live this way, won't the world continue to loot Christians? No, because the police will execute justice.

In a functioning government, the police will arrest people who steal your bike, even if you're a Christian. That is the nature of what is described in Romans 13. Nations that pride themselves on morality don't like the church, usually because the church proclaims that morality cannot save you from hell—it's not impressive to God. A totalitarian state hates the church because the church's members worship Jesus Christ—not their dictator. So, governments eventually turn on the church. But in the meantime, governments protect the church, not intentionally, but just by virtue of protecting their citizens.

That is the blessing of living in a Romans 13 world. We receive reward from government for doing good, we are protected by government from many harms, and we receive justice from government when we *are* harmed. Romans 12 calls for Christians not to repay evil. Romans 13 says you don't have to repay evil for evil, because God will take care of you through the government. Paul makes a pretty obvious point, however, that the government is not going to protect you if you're rebelling against it. If you want the Romans 13 protection, then don't rebel against the government.

Government benefits the church because (when doing what it should) it checks evil, and the church benefits government because (when doing what they should) Christians are good citizens. If both sides realize this, they come to a kind of harmony, a functional truce that can operate well, even in Nero's Rome.

LIMITS TO THE IMPERATIVES

This does not mean that harmony will reign forever or that it's reigning now. Even though you're supposed to submit to government, there are limits to the imperatives.

LIMIT #1: COMMANDS TO SIN

The first limit is the government cannot legitimately command you to commit sin. For example, the government cannot command you to steal or to worship an idol. Almost everyone knows the story of Shadrach, Meshach, and Abednego. In this real-world example of government oppression, Nebuchadnezzar commanded Hananiah, Mishael, and Azariah (their Hebrew names) to worship an oversized idol (Dan. 3:14). That was a direct command to sin, and they were right to disobey. This scenario may sound farfetched to American believers, but it's not farfetched in different parts of the world, where persecution is a reality for believers. If the Bible commands you not to do something that the government commands you to do, don't do it. Civil disobedience is the correct path in the face of clear-cut commandments to sin.

LIMIT #2: IGNORING BIBLICAL COMMANDS

Second, the government can't legitimately tell you to refrain from doing something God commands (James 4:17). For example, the Bible tells believers to congregate and worship together (e.g., Heb. 10:25; 1 Cor. 11:33). If the government says you cannot do that, then that prohibition would be invalid. The same would be true if the government tells churches not to sing. Paul commands believers in Ephesians 5:19 to sing to one another and to the Lord with psalms, hymns, and spiritual songs. In fact, the call to sing may very well be the Bible's most frequent command.[7] So if the government prohibited Christians from singing, we understand that our first obligation is to obey God, and that such a prohibition would not be a "lawful" command. The government cannot prohibit something that is a positive moral virtue or a command of Scripture.

LIMIT #3: CHURCH INFRINGEMENT

Third, the government cannot legitimately infringe on the function of the church. This is because of the embassy-like nature of the church. American believers are citizens of two kingdoms: the United States, and heaven.

In most places, those two circles overlap harmoniously. So, when the Jewish leaders brought Jesus the coin with Caesar's image on it and asked whether paying it to Caesar would be worshiping a false god, Jesus said, *Listen, get your two circles sorted out. Give to God what belongs to God; give to Caesar what belongs to Caesar.* The more you define those two circles, the freer you are to operate in this world.

These two circles overlap, but they do not interlock. The government cannot regulate the affairs of the church—that's outside its domain. Christ established the church; the Bible is the guide for the church; the elders are the leaders of the church under the authority of Jesus Christ. The government cannot regulate how often you worship or what your worship looks like. When the government tries to do this, it exceeds its authority.

In America, the Baptist tradition (among others) understands the government does not have the authority to regulate or interfere with the affairs of the church. We don't flaunt that; we try to operate in such a way that the government leaves us alone so we can "live quietly," "mind [our] own affairs," "work with our hands," and let the gospel go forward into the world (1 Thess. 4:10–11). We don't want to provoke a showdown; we just want to lead quiet lives, being good witnesses to our neighbors.

There are several biblical examples of government interfering with the church—and of the apostles responding. When the leaders of the Sanhedrin arrested Peter and John after these apostles healed a cripple and preached the gospel, they solemnly charged Peter and John to speak no more to anyone in Jesus's name. The apostles answered in Acts 4:19–21:

> "Whether it is right in the sight of God to listen to you rather than to God, you must judge, for we cannot but speak of what we have seen and heard." And when they had further threatened them, they let them go, finding no way to punish them, because of the people, for all were praising God for what had happened.

In essence, they say, *If it's right for you to say something that contradicts God, that's between you and the Lord. We're not going to tell you it's wrong. As for us, we're going to listen to God.* Later, in Acts 5, Peter and John started preaching again and got thrown in the slammer. During their trial, the high priest questioned them, saying, "We strictly charged you not to teach in this name, yet here you have filled Jerusalem with your teaching, and you intend to bring this man's blood upon us" (Acts 5:28). And in the next verse, Peter answered, "We must obey God rather than men."

A fourth limit on government authority kicks in when the mandate of the law contradicts God's purposes for laws. You have freedom when the purpose of a law goes against the reason God established government. (This limitation dovetails with our prudential motivation for obeying government, covered earlier in this chapter.)

For example, the white vehicle law would be nonsensical, because it is not evil to drive a dark-colored van or a red sports car. God did not institute government to dictate your vehicle selection. This sort of law does not check evil, nor does it promote moral good. Therefore, you don't have to obey it. But you should consider obeying it anyway for the sake of prudence or of your conscience.

Or take the ordinance in Gainesville, Georgia, that says you must eat fried chicken with your fingers—no utensils allowed.[8] Now, if you find yourself in Gainesville, and you eat fried chicken with a fork and a knife, you're not disobeying God. God allows you to eat fried chicken with utensils, even if you're in a locale that bans it. That's not why God made the government. That law doesn't check evil or promote the common good. However, you should seriously consider using your fingers so you don't get in trouble with the law or so your conscience doesn't convict you.

Although some government overreaches are pre-posterous, as a rule, we should not disobey government just to show its limits. Scripture does not instruct believers to expose how ridiculous some laws are, but it does call us to live harmoniously. We should generally comply with the laws of the land, even when we recognize that some laws go too far. We should keep exceptions to the rule *exceptional*.

There is a long Christian heritage that comes with this school of thought. Thomas Manton, who was Oliver Cromwell's government chaplain, wrote,

> Whatever God commandeth, I am bound to do it even in secret, though it be to my absolute prejudice; but now submission to man may be performed by suffering the penalty, though the obedience required be forborne; and in some cases a man may do contrary in private, where the thing is indifferent, and there is no danger of scandal and contempt of authority. Well, then, hear no voice but God's in your consciences, no doctrines in the church but Christ's.[9]

In other words, if God commands you to do something, you do it at all times, even in secret. But not if the government commands obedience to silly laws that don't check evil or promote good. In some cases, a man may violate such a law in private to avoid any danger of scandal or contempt for authority. You can neglect to obey the command and still be a good subject who is willing to go to jail for it.

Bhutan has a law that all Bhutanese citizens must wear a uniform when they're in public. Men have one style; women have another. Some question whether believers should wear their uniforms when they illegally gather for church. Some of them do, and some don't. No one from the government is there. The uniform law does not promote righteousness or check evil. So, in God's sight they're free to wear or not wear the uniform. Many people do not wear it—they reason that if the government has banned their worship, it has ceased to regulate *what* they wear when they are illegally gathered. Others do wear it for the sake of their conscience, and so they don't get in trouble with the government. It's one less thing to try to hide when they're in church. But it's a gray area, and they don't judge each other. That's what Manton is talking about. In private, it's not going to be scandalous. You have freedom to obey or not.

John Calvin argued that it was permissible to obey a morally neutral law, so long as we did not allow that law to bind our conscience, because only God's word should bind our conscience. He went even further and wrote that "our obligation to submit to laws looks to the purpose of law and not to the laws themselves."[10] In other words, you're not obliged to obey the silly laws. You look to the purpose of law, to what promotes common good and checks evil. Only those laws should bind the conscience and compel obedience.

Charles Hodge, an American Presbyterian theologian and principal of Princeton Theological Seminary in the nineteenth century, captured this understanding of Romans 13 very well. He wrote,

> When the civil government may be, and ought to be disobeyed, is one which every man must decide for himself.

It is a matter of private judgment. Every man must answer for himself to God, and therefore, every man must judge for himself, whether a given act is sinful or not. Daniel judged for himself. So did Shadrach, Meshach, and Abednego. So did the Apostles, and so did the martyrs.

An unconstitutional law or commandment is a nullity; no man sins in disregarding it. He disobeys, however, at his peril.[11]

How that echoes Romans 13! If the government makes an unconstitutional law, and you break it, you're not sinning. But you break it at your own risk. This is why Hodge says that obedience is a matter left to individuals: different Christians will navigate these decisions differently. Some might see a certain law as the government's valid exercise of God-given authority, while other Christians may disagree. Some Christians may not be willing to suffer the consequences for violating a law, and so they obey. Still others may have a more sensitive conscience. Far from being a problem, that diversity is actually a testimony to the fact that every believer stands before the Lord, not before other believers. (In fact, that is the very next principle Paul teaches, in Romans 14:1–5.)

CONCLUSION

Peter summed up New Testament ethics well enough when he said "We must obey God rather than men" (Acts 5:29). When the government leaves us alone, we have the ability to preach the gospel to the world, as Peter and John were doing, which is what God has commanded us to do. By extension, Scripture commands us to meet, worship, fellowship, and scatter into the world to bring the good news of Jesus Christ. In this era, we recognize that God's domain over this world is not expressed through a nation but through his church and the spread of the gospel. But the citizens of the kingdom of heaven are still citizens on earth, subject to the earth's empires. We ought to be good subjects, knowing that if we're good citizens we receive a reward, and if we're bad citizens we receive a punishment. That punishment can be severe, because God gave the government the sword. And we should never disobey flippantly, as even ungodly leaders can serve God's purposes for government to punish evil and promote the good.

By God's design, all countries have a virtuous function in God's sovereign plan: they check evil and fulfill God's purposes. This is regardless of the actual morality or virtue of any particular nation or leadership. Consequently, patriotism and service to one's country are, in a sense, virtuous, regardless of the virtue of the country in which you reside.

Christians, therefore, have the exact same responsibilities in a righteous society as they do in an *un*righteous one. These responsibilities include contributing to making their country as good as it can be. *Good*, however, is defined by God—not by human rulers. We hope both definitions overlap, but too often they do not.

Jesus acknowledged that Pilate's authority came from his heavenly Father. May we do the same, respecting our government's authority, while recognizing that its authority is limited, and that God alone is owed absolute allegiance.

————————————————

[1] Fred Pearce, "Urban Heat: Can White Roofs Help Cool World's Warming Crisis," e360, Yale School of the Environment, March 7, 2018, https://e360.yale.edu/features/urban-heat-can-white-roofs-help-cool-the-worlds-warming-cities.

[2] "The Easy Fix That Isn't: White Roofs May Increase Global Warming," Climate Control, October 31, 2011, https://www.climatecentral.org/blogs/white-roofs-may-increase-global-warming.

[3] Pearce, "Urban Heat."

[4] Augsburg Confession of Faith, Article XVI, 6–7.

[5] Westminster Confession of Faith, 23:4.

[6] A Christian's resistance may not always be peaceful, such as in an armed conflict between a just civil authority and an unjust civil authority—even if the just authority governs a smaller sphere. The justification for resistance in such cases rests on a doctrine known as "the doctrine of the lesser magistrate," developed by the princes of Germany in consultation with Martin Luther.

[7] Bob Kauflin suggests there are four hundred indirect references to singing and another fifty direct commands for believers to worship God through corporate song. See Bob Kauflin, "What Happens When We Sing," Desiring God, 2008 (https://www.desiringgod.org/messages/words-of-wonder-what-happens-when-we-sing).

[8] Ben Gerber, "The 10 Strangest Laws in Georgia," Enjuris, September 1, 2020, https://www.enjuris.com/blog/ga/strange-laws-in-georgia/.

[9] Thomas Manton, *The Complete Works of Thomas Manton* IV.iv (London: James Nisbet & Co., 1871), https://ccel.org/ccel/manton/manton04/manton04.vii.html.

[10] John Calvin, *Institutes of the Christian Religion*, Book IV, Chapter 10, para. 5. Author's own translation.

[11] Charles Hodge, *Systematic Theology* III.9 (Grand Rapids: Wm. B. Eerdmans Publishing Co., 1940), https://www.ccel.org/ccel/hodge/theology3/theology3.i.html.

3

JOY AMID INJUSTICE

Whoever keeps a command will know no evil thing, and
the wise heart will know the proper time and the just
way. For there is a time and a way for everything,
although man's trouble lies heavy on him.

— Ecclesiastes 8:5–6

A creek runs through my backyard, and next to it
sits a large pond. When we moved into our house, my wife
and I were excited about having the pond, but once grandparents visited us, they informed us that it represented a
mortal danger to our (at the time) three-year-old and one-
year-old daughters. It was obvious, the grandparents told
us, the pond had to go.

So, my father-in-law and I commenced "Operation:
Drain the Pond." We began at one end of the pond, where
the water trickled out to rejoin the creek. We dug out a

channel, laboring to increase the water flow in order to decrease the pond's water level. It took several days of hard labor, but we dug a channel three feet deep, which lowered the water level accordingly. (It wasn't lost on me that the three-foot channel was perhaps more dangerous than the pond itself, but we pressed on.)

Next, we turned our attention to the other end of the pond. We set out on a Lewis-and-Clark-style expedition to find the source of the water. We tracked the inflow uphill, through the woods, and found a series of smaller ponds and lesser streams—all working together to fill our pond. We chain-sawed fallen trees that were diverting current toward our pond, and we trenched, blocked, and pointed every drop of this wayward water away from our pond and back on its journey toward the great Potomac River. Eventually we found where the water had originally been directed away from the creek and toward our pond. A tree had fallen about a quarter-mile upstream, and its shift had diverted some of the water. If we could only move that tree, then we would deprive our pond of its water source, thereby ending the menace once and for all.

We worked for a week to move this fallen tree and to starve the pond. At one point my neighbor, who grew up along this creek, asked us, "You do realize that there are fallen trees all up and down this creek, right?" Never mind, we thought. This is the tree, right here. At one point, a friend told us he could bring a pump over and drain our pond in about twenty minutes. We declined; by then we were committed to the integrity of the operation.

Our efforts paid off. Eventually, we lowered the water level five feet and were feeling good about it. We had moved the tree upstream, and we admired the channel we had dug downstream. We had drained all the ponds that fed ours. Not an ounce of water remained. Mission accomplished.

Then the unthinkable happened—it rained. And rained. And rained. I watched our pond refill. To my shock, water was pouring into the pond—from downstream! The water from the creek was flowing backward into our pond, and all the channels we had built served only to refill the lesser ponds upstream. All our work had the opposite of its intended effect: it simply allowed the ponds to refill faster.

What was our mistake? We had read the entire situation backward. We thought the source was upstream, when it was downstream. We thought making the ponds easier to drain would help, but it really just increased water flow to our pond. Our five feet of water returned, and then some.

We realized that day there was no victory over the ponds and streams in our backyard. Our efforts proved futile because we had wrongly identified cause and effect.

CAUSE AND EFFECT

Humanity is prone to waging unwinnable battles fueled by misunderstanding cause and effect. Often, when confronted with injustice in this world, we read the situation backward. We assume present injustice is spawned and fed by previous sins—which, in many cases, is true.

But we can be quick to identify present solutions to historical problems in an attempt to mitigate future injustice. Too often, those endeavors have the opposite effect. Rather than addressing historical wrongs, they too easily only facilitate future injustice.

Perhaps no one grasped this concept better than Israel's King Solomon, the author of the books of Proverbs and Ecclesiastes.

The book of Proverbs equips you to navigate life on a straight and narrow path. When you understand Proverbs, you understand how to acquire wisdom and apply it to life situations in a God-honoring way. The book's main message is that acquiring wisdom is all-important: "The beginning of wisdom is this: Get wisdom, and whatever you get, get insight" (Prov. 4:7).

Ironically, its sequel, Ecclesiastes, helps you understand that acquiring all the wisdom under heaven cannot change reality, alter human nature, or satisfy the longing in man's heart to have significance in this world. The last verse of Ecclesiastes reads: "The end of the matter; all has been heard. Fear God and keep his commandments, for this is the whole duty of man. For God will bring every deed into judgment, with every secret thing, whether good or evil" (Eccles. 12:13–14).

Together, Proverbs and Ecclesiastes repeatedly emphasize wisdom's double benefit: with wisdom, you become more like God, and, you tend to accumulate life's joys instead of—or despite—life's disappointments.

Pursuing wisdom enables you to apply God's principles to the various areas of your life, such as family, career, finances, and even how Christians should relate to government. Perhaps the simplest way to understand how Proverbs and Ecclesiastes relate is this: Proverbs teaches how to avoid injustice. Ecclesiastes teaches that we won't always be successful in that attempt.

In fact, Ecclesiastes 8 focuses on how wise believers should operate in a fallen, unjust world.

Leading up to that chapter, Solomon highlights injustices and the futility they seem to carry, with thoughts like this:

> For what happens to the children of man and what happens to the beasts is the same; as one dies, so dies the other. They all have the same breath, and man has no advantage over the beasts, for all is vanity. (Eccles. 3:19)

Solomon understood that injustice isn't merely existential. Right now, the unjust seem to prosper, often with the aid of government. Injustice can be terribly practical, common, and entrenched in human affairs:

> If you see in a province the oppression of the poor and the violation of justice and righteousness, do not be amazed at the matter, for the high official is watched by a higher, and there are yet higher ones over them. But this is gain for a land in every way: a king committed to cultivated fields. (Eccles. 5:8–9)

Here Solomon gives one reason for a fact Moses had earlier identified and that Jesus would later affirm: "There will never cease to be poor in the land" (Deut. 15:11;

Mark 14:7). Evil in society is often systemic, resulting from decisions made by officials higher up the ladder than we perceive. Moral good is also systemic. A king committed to cultivated fields instead of overgrown and unplowed fields will cause blessings to trickle down throughout society.

Having exposed the brokenness of this world, Solomon then focuses on where many people do: on government as a solution for injustice in the world. This makes sense—within limits. Similar to the draining of my pond, government can make short-term changes to limit injustice. In fact, this is precisely what it was designed to do. But these changes are just that: short-term. Limited. Government is not able to address the root cause of injustice.

Mankind's ultimate problem, and the very source of injustice in society, is sin. Our infectiously rebellious hearts are the cause of sin's proliferation. Thus, the ultimate solution to injustice is the gospel. But when sinners repent and place their faith in the substitutionary death of Jesus and believe in the power of his resurrection, they are reconciled to God. Sin holds no dominion over followers of Christ (Rom. 6:14). Thus, the gospel remains the only way to address the root cause of injustice in society.

That is not to say that injustice doesn't matter or that people should be passive in the face of it. On the contrary, Solomon proposes a conundrum—that government itself is a secondary source of injustice in the world. Thus, government is both a perpetrator of unrighteousness as well as one of the most important means given to people to *check* unrighteousness. To that extent, just government is an imperfect but helpful solution to worldly injustice, which is what God established government to be (Gen. 9:6).

This recognition—that government is a secondary source of evil but also has the capacity to *check* the evil that is in the world—is what leads to Ecclesiastes 8. There, Solomon describes how good government can remedy the evils of bad government. Solomon begins Ecclesiastes 8 with a triad of axiomatic truth: power, structure, and authority exist. You see this in these words:

> Keep the king's command, *because of God's oath to him.* Be not hasty to go from his presence. Do not take your stand in an evil cause, for he does whatever he pleases. For the word of the king is supreme, and who may say to him, "What are you doing?" Whoever keeps a command will know no evil thing, and the wise heart will know the proper time and the just way. For there is a time and a way for everything, although man's trouble lies heavy on him. (Eccles. 8:2–6, emphasis added)

The phrase *because of God's oath to him* sounds confusing. The Complete Jewish Bible translates it *"because of the oath before God."* It's hard to tell if Solomon means God's oath to the king—presumably a reference to Genesis 9—or Israel's oath to serve Solomon (1 Chron. 29:24). Either way, Solomon's point here is that this oath should motivate our obedience to government's commands.

The righteous regularly live in this interwoven oath, knowing God has established government in the world to check evil—to protect our freedom of worship, our family structure, our food supply, and life itself (see chapter 1 of this book). God called people to worship him, to "be fruitful and multiply," to cultivate the earth, and to protect human life (Gen. 9:1–6). At the same time, God ordained government to protect what he called humans to strive for.

We need to explore how government—the very institution God appointed and armed to check evil—can become the source of injustice, and how Christians should respond when it does.

POWER STRUGGLES

God chartered government to protect citizens in four areas (worship, family, food, justice), and God empowered government to be forceful in its protective role. Government is the one institution God armed to do its job. When Paul commands obedience to rulers in Romans 13, his words imply armed confrontation for violations: "For rulers are not a terror to good conduct, but to bad. Would you have no fear of the one who is in authority?" (Rom. 13:3).

This is not a mere rhetorical question. When you fear being cuffed and thrown in jail, you obey. Whether Herod is the governor or David is the king, whether your political hero or your worst nightmare sits in the Oval Office, each has a police force and the military to compel compliance, and they are not afraid to use them.

The motivation to obey the government, however, finds its most compelling reason in Paul's foundation: "Let every person be subject to the governing authorities. For there is no authority except from God, and those that exist have been instituted by God" (Rom. 13:1). God is the one who gave government its mandate and the power to enforce it.

Solomon's words in Ecclesiastes 8 and Paul's in Romans 13 seem to be sourced from the same outline—but from different angles. Solomon emphasizes the righteous citizen's oath of obedience; Paul stresses God's empowerment of the ruler. But neither Paul, writing as a converted Jew under Roman occupation, nor Solomon, who reflected on injustice in Ecclesiastes 5 and 8, is saying that every edict from every king is just. Naiveté did not blind either biblical writer to his broken world.

Solomon's argument is practical: the king "does whatever he pleases. For the word of the king is supreme" (Eccles. 8:3–4). Solomon makes a simple argument to keep us out of handcuffs: God, who invented and armed government to enforce protections, is the one who is sovereign over governments, so you should probably listen to them. Otherwise, you may soon be measured for an orange jumpsuit.

Because Paul and Solomon have tag-teamed us into obeying the government, some believers may be tempted to put as much distance between themselves and the government as possible. But Solomon instructs us differently.

KINGS AND COUNSELORS

Often, people who ascend to significant leadership roles feel the weight of responsibility and surround themselves with advisors. Solomon did. So did Pharaoh and

Nebuchadnezzar. David kept Nathan the prophet nearby. But even in the counsel of supposed sages, wisdom plays hide and seek—revealing just how scarce wisdom can be.

Do you remember when Nebuchadnezzar had troubling dreams and asked his cabinet-level soothsayers to tell him what they meant? They fell helpless on their faces, unable to discern truth. God used their helplessness to position Daniel to be the lone voice of wisdom. Generations earlier, God did something similar with Pharaoh, whose advisors were hopeless in the face of dream interpretation. Joseph stood out because he showed supernatural wisdom—a river of practical knowledge that flowed from God's mind to his. Joseph's wisdom elevated him before Pharaoh.

Eight hundred years later, when Absalom staged a coup against his father, King David, Absalom took some of David's counselors as part of the booty. The problem was that those counselors had flunked out of wisdom training, and once Absalom took their advice, he fell out of power, and David reclaimed the throne. Solomon, the wisest king in Israel's history, learned from Absalom's example, and surrounded himself with wise counselors. That set up his son Rehoboam for success—except Solomon's successor chose not to listen to wise counsel, and he started a civil war.

We see it play out over and over: the wisest leaders recognize they are not wise enough, so they surround themselves with sages. The foolish ones have not taken advice since they were toddlers, so they go it alone or surround themselves with fools who pontificate hot air. Wisdom in the corridors of power is rare.

So, if you find yourself in the presence of a high-ranking government authority, listen to Solomon's advice, and stay for a minute:

> Be not hasty to go from his presence. Do not take your stand in an evil cause, for he does whatever he pleases. (Eccles. 8:3)

Don't scan the room and plan a quick escape. Size things up. Get the lay of the land. See what is happening there. If justice is being served, appreciate it. If injustice is occurring, take a breath and think it through. Don't dig in your heels and make a scene. After all, the king is going to do what the king is going to do. He has the power and the means to enforce his agenda.

Is God advising that we tolerate, ignore, or become accomplices to governmental injustice? Of course not. But then why does Solomon add, "Do not take your stand in an evil cause, for he does whatever he pleases" (Eccles. 8:3)?

Solomon's point is this: when you are in the presence of the authority, be cautious about how you confront him. Remember, throughout Ecclesiastes, Solomon is acknowledging things about human nature and society that will never change. Solomon knows that the ruler will do whatever he wants. This verse does not advise you to miss your opportunity to speak about injustice. It advises you to be careful about how you take your stand. Solomon says there is "a time for every matter under heaven" and "there is a time and a way for everything" (Eccles. 3:1, 8:6). Maybe this is your opportunity to make a bold but respectful stand. Maybe this is your time to speak softly and graciously. Maybe this is your time to listen so you'll be more equipped to find solutions later. Wisdom informs how you calculate your next move.

The picture is a little different in our American system of government because we are allowed to stand in front of the White House and say, "Are you out of your mind?" The US Constitution even protects our right to gather peacefully, picket, protest, and criticize our government. Speaking up will not doom you to Guantánamo Bay. Nevertheless, the biblical principle holds firm. You should think carefully about how you interact with those in power.

Solomon isn't saying you should never speak up. He *is* telling you to navigate troubled waters carefully: "The wise heart will know the proper time and the just way" (Eccles. 8:5b). Jesus applied the same principle when telling his disciples how to speak before the authorities:

> Behold, I am sending you out as sheep in the midst of wolves, so be wise as serpents and innocent as doves. Beware of men, for they will deliver you over to courts and flog you in their synagogues, and you will be dragged before governors and kings for my sake, to bear witness before them and the Gentiles. When they deliver you over, do not be anxious how you are to speak or what you are to say, for what you are to say will be given to you in that hour. For it is not you who speak, but the Spirit of your Father speaking through you. (Matt. 10:16–20)

If you find yourself in a position to influence a civil authority, let wisdom guide you to discern the right thing to say at the right time.

This advice may cause you discomfort—especially if you're fed up with Christians keeping silent when they *should* speak up—but stick with me.

GOD ALLOWS INJUSTICE

Solomon isn't writing these words to us from the tranquil isolation of the palace library. He is fully aware of injustice in the world: "All this I observed while applying my heart to all that is done under the sun, when man had power over man to his hurt" (Eccles. 8:9). Not much has changed in three thousand years. People still harm each other.

Years ago, I saw injustice play out firsthand when I served as chaplain for the Los Angeles County Sheriff's Department. In 2008, a string of robberies led to the arrest, trial, and sentencing of Ruben Martinez—a man who had a strong alibi. Martinez was convicted and sentenced to forty years in prison.

Eleven years into his sentence, a new district attorney put fresh eyes on the case and discovered suppressed video evidence that verified Martinez's alibi. He was at work when the crimes were committed, not at the crime scene. The government attorneys had withheld the evidence, and the defense attorney was not real keen on doing his job. The new district attorney took interest, though, and Ruben Martinez was exonerated after more than a decade in prison for a crime he did not commit.[1]

At his press conference, Martinez explained he had become a Christian while in prison. His wife, who prayed for him throughout the ordeal, also gave her heart to Jesus. Martinez explained that he was not angry at God or the government. God had brought himself glory—even in the face of injustice.

Jackie Lacey, the district attorney who oversaw Martinez's exoneration, said upon his release, "Although the vast majority of convictions are correctly upheld ... at times the pursuit of justice is not perfect. And Mr. Martinez's case serves as a stark reminder to all of us: despite our best efforts, we don't always get it right."[2] Tragically, in the Martinez case, the problem was not one of accidentally overlooking evidence. People in authority did their level-best *not* to get it right.

Ruben Martinez's case is not an isolated example of injustice. Take a fresh look at the last century or so when lynchings were not isolated incidents, but common. Expand your view to look back at government-sponsored injustices in every era: Communism's more than 100 million victims[3] (in former Soviet countries and still rising in China, Cuba, Laos, North Korea, Vietnam and elsewhere[4]), Nazi Germany's holocaust of 11 million souls (including 6 million Jews),[5] the Ottoman Empire's genocide against a million Armenians,[6] the Inquisition and the Reformation wars, the executions under Muhammad,[7] Rome's multiple persecutions of Christians under several emperors—and on and on. Three thousand years before the Martinez case, Solomon warned, "All this I observed while applying my heart to all that is done under the sun, when man had power over man to his hurt" (Eccles. 8:9).

That's right. Even within the power structures of God-ordained government, injustice abounds.

Just when you thought Solomon had painted the darkest view of injustice, he splashes more gore on his canvas: "Then I saw the wicked buried. They used to go in and out of the holy place and were praised in the city where they had done such things. This also is vanity" (Eccles. 8:10). You read that right; wicked people were praised for their wickedness. It almost feels like Solomon is looking into a crystal ball and foretelling America's political present. We repeatedly watch our elected officials fail personally and in policymaking. Their missteps are measured over their careers as they somehow cling to power for decades. If they worked at Home Depot and recommended a power-washer as the perfect tool to rewire a house, how long would they wear the orange Home Depot vest? Were they surgeons who consistently confused left and right, how long would they remain in practice? Yet often government not only tolerates incompetence but even rewards it.

Solomon observed that conundrum: people in power seem to be insulated from consequence. When they die, tributes on media outlets make them sound more honorable than George Washington, and the government will order flags to be flown at half-staff.

Worse still, even when justice is eventually served, its delay encourages more evil: "Because the sentence against an evil deed is not executed speedily, the heart of the children of man is fully set to do evil" (Eccles. 8:11). In Solomon's day, delayed consequences emboldened evil deeds. People added evil act to evil act because others appeared to get away with it. The apparent lack of punishment enticed people to join the sin circus.

This remains true today. Remember that in the same instant God established government, he entrusted government with the authority to use capital punishment to deter violence: "Whoever sheds the blood of man, by man shall his blood be shed" (Gen. 9:6). In other words, if you choose to murder someone, you should be put to death. And Paul wrote that the ruler bears the sword against evildoers (Rom. 13:4). In our era, however, the death penalty is all but dead. Because of the appeals process, most executions occur 238 months—that's twenty years!—after the court pronounces the sentence.[8] And that's only an average, meaning many executions for murder and other capital crimes are delayed even longer.

Injustice happens, even from within government. It occurred in Solomon's day, and three thousand intervening years of human history shows a consistent pattern of abuse. You and I should do what we can to prevent it; we should elect virtuous people who will use government to keep evil at bay. But don't be surprised when you see it. Rest in this: God will judge every act of evil.

THE JUST JUDGE

God has a perspective that you and I are not privy to: he knows what is going on behind the scenes. Solomon's wisdom allowed him to reveal the distinction between life on earth and eternal life:

Though a sinner does evil a hundred times and prolongs his life, yet I know that it will be well with those who fear God, because they fear before him. But it will not be well with the wicked, neither will he prolong his days like a shadow, because he does not fear before God. (Eccles. 8:12–13)

The thought almost seems contradictory. The wicked person sees his earthly life stretch out beyond the sunset, but when he dies, he goes to hell, being eternally separated from God, in whose presence is perfect justice. God will call him to account for all of his wickedness.

Solomon preempts a tough question here: If God is sovereign over government, and government acts in an unjust way, doesn't that mean God is acting in an unjust way? Solomon seems to have one hand on his hip as he says, "That's what it looks like!" If we are honest, we can struggle with this one, too. We believe that God is in charge, and God put the elected officials in positions of authority. When these leaders—appointed by God—do wicked things or pass evil legislation, who is ultimately responsible? The evildoers are. But does God, who granted the mantle of power, bear any part of the injustice?

Your theological gut will tell you, "No way!" James shut this door with one statement: "For God cannot be tempted with evil" (James 1:13b). Scripture tells us in no uncertain terms that God will judge injustice:

I will draw near to you for judgment. I will be a swift witness against the sorcerers, against the adulterers, against those who swear falsely, against those who oppress the hired worker in his wages, the widow and the fatherless, against those who thrust aside the sojourner, and do not fear me, says Yahweh of hosts. (Mal. 3:5)

God will remember every innocent person who was sentenced to prison and every innocent person who was executed. More than that, God will remember all those who are responsible for injustice, and he will judge them.

God temporarily allows evil to prosper because he is using the brokenness of our world for his own greater purposes—purposes we cannot see in the present. Think about the great injustices Joseph's brothers thrust upon Joseph. Why did God allow him to be betrayed and sold into slavery? God's ultimate priority in Joseph's life was bigger than the injustice he permitted. God used injustice to establish Israel in Egypt to set up the Exodus, which demonstrated once and for all that Israel was a people called by God and set apart from the nations of the earth. God was at work, but Joseph had no idea about the role God had called him to play. He was looking at the underside of the tapestry of his life, unaware of how his sovereign God was weaving a story of deliverance through a series of personal injustices.

In Ecclesiastes 3, Solomon addressed the sovereignty of God in more than a dozen pendulum statements of "a time to _____, and a time to _____." You have heard them a thousand times:

> For everything there is a season, and a time for every
> matter under heaven:
> a time to be born, and a time to die;
> a time to plant, and a time to pluck up what is planted;
> a time to kill, and a time to heal;

a time to break down, and a time to build up;

a time to weep, and a time to laugh;

a time to mourn, and a time to dance;

a time to cast away stones, and a time to gather stones together;

a time to embrace, and a time to refrain from embracing;

a time to seek, and a time to lose;

a time to keep, and a time to cast away;

a time to tear, and a time to sew;

a time to keep silence, and a time to speak;

a time to love, and a time to hate;

a time for war, and a time for peace. (Eccles. 3:1–8)

A nihilist or atheist might read this and deduce that nothing has meaning—we are all participants in an impersonal universe; we are just matter in motion, they might say. But Solomon closes off that interpretation with his introduction, where he declares that God is sovereign over "every matter under heaven" (Eccles. 3:1). It is God who has set the limits of seasons and suffering. It is God who has appointed both prosperity and war. By verses 10–11, Solomon hits his climax:

> I have seen the business that God has given to the children of man to be busy with. He has made everything beautiful in its time. Also, he has put eternity into man's heart, yet so that he cannot find out what God has done from the beginning to the end. (Eccles. 3:10–11)

You may not like Solomon's conclusion, but you should at least understand it: God does not always clue us in on what he is doing. This applies even more when an almighty God allows injustice. When Joseph was sold by his brothers, God was working. When he was falsely accused by Potiphar's wife, God was working. When he languished in prison, God was working. When he was reunited with his brothers, God was working. But God did not pull Joseph aside and show him the blueprint and say, "Hang in there, buddy. I am carrying out a plan." God was silent during the multiple stages of personal injustice.

We want to understand. We see people who are wronged by injustice, and we want to know what God is up to. Solomon reminds us that sometimes we do not get to know. But in his perfect timing, "God will judge the righteous and the wicked, for there is a time for every matter and for every work" (Eccles. 3:17); for "he has made everything beautiful in its time" (Eccles. 3:11).

UNTIL THEN

Injustice should sadden us as compassionate humans. It saddened Solomon. It made him almost pull his hair out. In fact, the more he studied his broken world, the more melancholy he became. Solomon navigated toward brutal honesty that says our lives are insignificant in the face of injustice.

You work hard, you study hard, you love hard. You give your life in service to your country, to your family, to your church, to your job—and wickedness will not only continue to exist; it will increase. Shouldn't your life have a greater impact?

It should, and it will, if you're measuring with God's metrics. If you spend your life trying to reduce government corruption and beat government back into the sandbox God marked out for it in Genesis 9, then you will have done a good thing. But if you measure your life by your success in that effort, you will be disappointed.

Remember, Solomon ends Ecclesiastes by concluding that surrender and obedience to God is man's duty. We don't need to overcomplicate God's metrics:

> The end of the matter; all has been heard. Fear God and keep his commandments, for this is the whole duty of man. For God will bring every deed into judgment, with every secret thing, whether good or evil. (Eccles. 12:13–14)

You can spend your life trying to right the wrongs in this world. You may win some victories, but you will never make the world a place where justice reigns. Only God can do that—and he will when he establishes his kingdom on earth. Meanwhile, we should take joy in the good work God has set before us. As Solomon writes,

> I saw that there is nothing better than that a man should rejoice in his work, for that is his lot. (Eccles. 3:22)

> Behold, what I have seen to be good and fitting is to eat and drink and find enjoyment in all the toil with which one toils under the sun the few days of his life that God has given him, for this is his lot. (Eccles. 5:18).

God's gift to people is the ability to enjoy what we can along the journey, even though injustice prevails in parts of our world.

The general rule Solomon is applying is that we should make our lives a bastion where people can find joy, despite the existence of evil under the sun. As far as you are able, live a quiet and joyful life, spreading that joy to all people God has called you to do life with.

Meanwhile, finding joy in our journey does not call us to be blind to injustice around us. Quite the opposite! Scripture commands us, "Open your mouth for the mute, for the rights of all who are destitute. Open your mouth, judge righteously, defend the rights of the poor and needy" (Prov. 31:8–9). When you are confronted with injustice, rectify it if you can. If you see someone being abused, stand in the gap. God called you to defend the powerless. This will bring you joy, because "a desire fulfilled is sweet to the soul, but to turn away from evil is an abomination to fools" (Prov. 13:19).

Speak up for the oppressed. Correct whatever injustices are in your purview. Wisdom will guide you to act when God is behind it, but folly will trick you into taking on the weight of this world's injustice—something only Christ can bear.

SURRENDER

Look no further than the Gospels for the ultimate example of a righteous man taking joy in his work despite the injustices all around him. It was multiple layers of injustice that resulted in the government-sanctioned murder of Jesus.

The Lord Jesus Christ is the picture of divine trust in the face of injustice. He was stricken, smitten, rejected by those he came to save, betrayed, denied, abandoned, mocked, beaten, crowned with thorns—and then crucified.

One justice system knowingly leveled false charges against him. Another recognized the charges as false yet did nothing, washing its hands of him. The witnesses were bribed. The trial was a kangaroo court. The appeals process was flawed, and the result was that the innocent Jesus was executed alongside convicted felons. His example of enduring injustice compels us to meet him in the surrender to God that says "Father, if you are willing, remove this cup from me. Nevertheless, not my will, but yours, be done" (Luke 22:42).

Such surrender forces us to long for the day when God will turn the tapestry over and let us see the beauty that he has been weaving into our world.

---

[1] Ken Otterbourg, "Ruben Martinez Jr.," National Registry of Exonerations, www.law.umich.edu/special/exoneration/Pages/casedetail.aspx?caseid=5635.

[2] Los Angeles County District Attorney's Office, "District Attorney Jackie Lacey's Conviction Review Unit Exonerates Los Angeles Man," November 12, 2019, https://da.lacounty.gov/sites/default/files/press/111219_District_Attorney_Jackie_Laceys_Conviction_Review_Unit_Exonerates_Los_Angeles_Man.pdf

[3] Victims of Communism Memorial Foundation, "About," accessed April 19, 2021, https://victimsofcommunism.org/about/.

[4] Victims of Communism Memorial Foundation, accessed April 19, 2021, https://victimsofcommunism.org/.

⁵ Andy Andrews, *How Do You Kill 11 Million People?* (n.p.: Thomas Nelson, 2012), https://www.lifeway.com/en/product/how-do-you-kill-11-million-people-P005481721.

⁶ United States Holocaust Memorial Museum, "The Armenian Genocide (1915–1916): Overview," Holocaust Encyclopedia, accessed April 21, 2021, https://encyclopedia.ushmm.org/content/en/article/the-armenian-genocide-1915-16-overview.

⁷ WikiIslam, "List of Killings Ordered or Supported by Muhammad," March 7, 2021, https://wikiislam.net/wiki/List_of_Killings_Ordered_or_Supported_by_Muhammad.

⁸ Statista, "Average time between sentencing and execution for inmates on death row in the United States from 1990 to 2018," accessed April 21, 2021, https://www.statista.com/statistics/199026/average-time-between-sentencing-and-execution-of-inmates-on-death-row-in-the-us/.

4

CITY OF MAN, KINGDOM OF GOD

Therefore render to Caesar the things that are Caesar's, and to God the things that are God's.

— Matthew 22:21

The sack of Rome in AD 410 is one of the most significant events of world history and was a critical stepping-stone to the fall of the Roman Empire in AD 476. Rome had ruled the earth for more than six hundred years. In her six centuries of global domination, Rome gave much of the world a unified language, currency, and culture. One seat of government spread its control over three continents. Unbeknownst to Caesar, Rome was literally paving the roads that missionaries would use to take the gospel global.

The Roman Empire had extended into Asia, parts of India, the Middle East, North Africa, the Mediterranean area, and much of Europe. Though its size waxed and waned with the centuries, Rome imposed a cohesive culture, worship of false gods, language, government, a bevy of laws, a taxation system, and a military. Its imprint was unrivaled.

Though Rome certainly wasn't a democracy at the time of its fall, it had many democratic tendencies. Romans believed that the actions of individual citizens could determine outcomes for the empire, which led them to blame social ills on one segment of the population. The empire posited, "We would have been fine if only *those* people had backed the government in *this* way."

As the church began to take root in the Roman Empire, this attribute of Roman politics became a serious problem for Christians. Many Romans believed that as more people worshiped Jesus, and therefore refused to worship Roman gods, the gods would become upset and punish Rome. So they started blaming Christians for everything unfavorable that happened in Rome. For example, in AD 64, Emperor Nero accused the Christians of setting Rome on fire, and he then persecuted them fiercely.

After many years of persecution, the Roman attitude toward Christianity softened. Emperor Constantine nominally converted to Christianity in AD 313, legalized the church, and endorsed Christianity as the religion of the Roman Empire.

Less than one hundred years later, Rome was sacked, and the empire soon came crashing down.

When invaders came knocking on Rome's door, Christianity became the obvious scapegoat. It is true that the Roman Empire's downfall was sealed once Christianity became its adopted religion—but not *because of* Christianity. Augustine argued this point in the early fifth century, just after Rome's capture, in his multivolume work called *The City of God*. Instead of apologizing for Christianity's contribution to Rome's demise, Augustine took the opportunity to expose the absurdity of Roman idolatry. He did this by naming the Roman gods and articulating the contradictory teachings of their priests. If Roman theology was unreliable, he argued, how could its spiritual leaders be trusted in matters of national interest? How could its fall be blamed on Christians, when the Roman idols so brazenly contradicted themselves?

No one would dispute that Rome had been tremendously successful, idols and all. They had unified much of the world and ushered in an unprecedented six centuries of stability. But Augustine argued that Rome's past successes were no more due to her paganism than her subsequent failures were due to Christianity. He waded into controversy by saying that the same holds true for every nation in history. He wrote that there is no such thing as a nation that rises or falls based upon the influence of Christianity. God—Augustine believed—is at work in nations to rein in evil, but a nation's rise or fall is not consequential to its connection to religion. Instead, "It rests with the decision of God in his just judgment and mercy either to afflict or console mankind, so that some wars come to an end more speedily, others more slowly."[1]

One of the many lessons from *The City of God* is that instead of fixating on a nation's religiosity, people should view the world as divided between two cities: the City of Man and the City of God. Significantly, Augustine argued that God's design was for his people to dwell simultaneously in *both* cities.

Take a moment to process that thought: God's people do indeed dwell in both cities. They're citizens of their own nation *and* citizens of heaven. In fact, Paul claimed Roman citizenship after his conversion (see Acts 16:37–38 and 22:25–29), and there is no evidence he understood those claims to conflict with his heavenly citizenship (e.g., Phil. 3:20).

Augustine argues that Christians cannot be blamed for the success or the failure of either one of the two cities—the City of Man or the City of God.[2] When the kingdom of God advances, the propellant has more to do with God's sovereign will than an abundance of Christian piety. Ultimately, the City of God is victorious over the City of Man. The earth will always fail, so people should think carefully about where they place their hope.

TWO SWORDS

The City of God sparked a consequential theological debate. Many misconstrued Augustine as advocating that both cities—the government and the church—should be under one sovereign's control. Thus, according to this view, Rome's problems began when Constantine moved the seat of his government out of Rome to Byzantium. Some argued that when this move took place, the City of

Man (government) was no longer in charge of the City of God (the church), thus weakening the Roman Empire.

In this understanding, Rome's downfall resulted from one person's failure to effectively control both the church and the government. The Roman Catholic Church bought into this idea and argued that both the City of God and the City of Man should fall under one kingdom and be led by one ruler. This eventually resulted in what became known as the Holy Roman Empire, which gave both political and ecclesiological power to the pope, who held authority over even the emperor.

This vision of how the City of Man and the City of God relate is often referred to as the Catholic doctrine of *utrumque gladium* (a Latin expression that translates *two swords*). This doctrine teaches that each city is ruled by its own sword, but one person ought to wield both. This doctrine was established by the Catholic Church with paragraph 1302 of the Catechism of the Catholic Church—the Bull *Unam Sanctam.* Here is the key part:

> For when the apostles said "Here are two swords" (Luke 22:38)—that is, in the Church, since it was the apostles who were speaking—the Lord did not answer, "It is too much," but "It is enough." Whoever denies that the temporal sword is in the power of Peter [the pope] does not properly understand the word of the Lord when He said: "Put up thy sword into the sheath" (John 18:11). Both swords, therefore, the spiritual and the temporal, are in the power of the Church. The former is to be used by the Church, the latter for the Church; the one by the hand of the priest, the other by the hand of kings and knights, but at the command and permission of the

priest. Moreover, it is necessary for one sword to be under the other, and the temporal authority to be subjected to the spiritual; for the apostle says, "For there is no power but of God: and the powers that be are ordained of God" (Rom. 13:1); but they would not be ordained unless one were subjected to the other, and, as it were, the lower made the higher by the other.[3]

With this design, the City of Man operates under the sword of law enforcement, taxation, the military, and other restrictive powers of government. The City of God operates under the sword of the sacraments. But key to the Catholic understanding of this doctrine is that one ruler should hold both swords.

This is why in the Middle Ages, knights often wore a crest with two swords, demonstrating they had a dual duty to enforce civil laws and to go on crusades to advance religious causes. Essentially, they worked for both cities under the authority of the pope, bearing one sword for law and another for the church. (Because no concept of separation of church and state existed, most knights would have struggled to articulate which sword they were wielding.)

Another image from this era features a two-headed eagle, grasping a sword in each of its talons. This crest was used by many patriarchs in the Roman Catholic, Russian Orthodox, and Greek Orthodox churches. Each church's papal leadership assumed legal authority to appoint political leaders and to persecute those who didn't fall in line with its ecclesiastical teaching. This image stands as a clear example of the doctrine of the two swords.

The doctrine of the two swords continues today in the Anglican Church, albeit in a mostly symbolic way. The Queen of England is the figurative head of both Great Britain and the Church of England, making her one person "ruling" with two swords over two cities.

DIFFERENT KINGDOMS

How ought we to understand the two-sword doctrine through the lens of Scripture? We must see that the New Testament does not call for one person to control both the government and the church. For example, Paul never sought political power but instead submitted himself to it (Acts 25:11). In fact, in Acts 28:19, Paul expressly notes that in terms of politics, he had no qualms with either the Jews or the Romans, even though in that passage the Jews were acting as opponents to the gospel. When he was on trial, Paul never told the governors or kings that they had better release him or else they would find themselves as enemies of the City of God. Instead, he submitted to their authority and availed himself of the legal process, all the while appealing for them to come to faith themselves (Acts 26:29–32; 28:19, 30–31). This should not surprise us, because, after all, that is the example of Jesus who said, "My kingdom is not of this world. If my kingdom were of this world, my servants would have been fighting, that I might not be delivered over to the Jews. But my kingdom is not from the world" (John 18:36).

Instead of appealing for the church to have authority over earthly nations, the New Testament calls for these two cities to exist side by side. They are separate and do not rule over each other, but as citizens, we find significant overlap.

As Christians, we are under the authority of the government and under the authority of God's word. Though we live under both authorities, each regulates different parts of our lives. The government regulates our taxes and our laws, while the word of God stands supreme, regulating our affections and our worship.

While I've made the case that the City of Man and the City of God are two different cities, please don't misunderstand; I'm not arguing that they are entirely separate. We as citizens live in both, and God himself is sovereign over both. As our supreme ruler, God regulates every area of our lives. But God rules over the worship of his people expressly (by his word), and he rules over the nations permissively (by providence). In other words, both cities fall under the lordship of Christ. Moreover, the civil authorities in the City of Man are to wield their authority in accordance with God's revealed purposes, design, and limitations.

This coin is two-sided, providing a clear authority boundary. Scripture does not lay out the granular details of what laws or tax codes we should have in the City of Man. That would be a conflation of the two cities. But Scripture does provide principles for godliness, justice, and righteousness that can be applied to government. Just as the church does not and should not possess the authority to regulate the government, the government does not and should not possess the authority to regulate the church. It cannot use the sword to dictate when or how the Christian church should worship. That authority belongs to God—not to Caesar.

In the meantime, Christians find themselves much as Augustine did: citizens of two kingdoms.

Think of it this way: each local church is an embassy where we can retreat from this world to worship God. We gather other citizens of heaven into the embassy of the City of God, which is situated within the City of Man (Acts 2:5; Rev. 5:9, 7:9). The City of Man does not have authority over the embassy, so it should not interfere with this gathering. Then, when corporate worship is over, we scatter into the City of Man to do the work of the ministry (Matt. 28:19; Mark 13:10; Eph. 4:11–14).

In this model, the Christian is always under authority, but God has established different streams of authority for each city. God rules his church through the preaching of his word. He does not use leaders in the City of Man to rule the worship of those in the City of God. Instead, as people come to faith in Christ, they submit their lives and their worship to the authority of Scripture. And they become dual citizens.

Simultaneously, God sovereignly rules the City of Man through providence and conscience as nations rise and fall. Through providence, he determines who sits on earthly thrones, while our consciences reveal God-given natural law that restrains sin. Providence and conscience are not experienced exclusively by those in the City of God; rather, even people who do not know the Lord or ascribe to the principles of the Bible have their sins restrained by their consciences, and everyone lives under civil authority that God has providentially allowed.

God's sovereignty over the City of Man does not exempt Christians from submitting to the authorities of the City of Man. Remember, the governor who punishes injustice and promotes goodness is operating within the scope and purpose of his God-given authority (Rom. 13:3–4), and "whoever resists" such authority "resists what God has appointed, and those who resist will incur judgment.... Therefore one must be in subjection, not only to avoid God's wrath but also for the sake of conscience" (Rom. 13:2, 5).

Nor does God's sovereignty over the City of Man exempt Christians from influencing our civil authorities. James wrote, "Whoever knows the right thing to do and fails to do it, for him it is sin" (James 4:17). Christians know (or *should* know—which is why I wrote this book!) better than anyone on earth the limited scope and purpose for which God established government: to administer justice and promote goodness (Gen. 9:6, Rom 13:2–5). Better yet, by giving us the Bible, God has equipped us to define *justice* and *goodness* biblically. Such revelation helps us to pinpoint God's perfect design for government—and to identify where civil authorities diverge from God's design. So, because the Christian "knows the right thing to do," he or she should communicate biblical principles of governance to the civil authorities and encourage them to operate within God's design, scope, and purpose for government.

The Bible is full of examples of God's people using their positions to communicate biblical principles to civil leaders. Even though the Bible does not rule the City of Man, God's word does encourage believers to confront un-just and immoral societal laws. John the Baptist stands as an early example of one leading the charge. Although no religious entity had installed Herod, John the Baptist con-fronted him anyway—on moral grounds. Though it cost him his head on a platter, he condemned Herod, saying it was sinful for him to marry his brother's wife (Mark 6:18).

However, the exposure citizens have to their civil leaders varies by form of government. The regime type most often depicted in Scripture is that of a monarchy. But this does not imply that the Bible recognizes *only* monar-chies. On the contrary, God's purposes for government are consistent, regardless of the particular form that govern-ment takes—be it a monarchy, democracy, or republic. When God instituted government in Genesis 9, he did so without specifying what form that government should take. Now, naturally, the circle of people positioned to influence a monarch is smaller than the circle of people positioned to influence, say, representatives of a post-En-lightenment Western democratic republic. Enter another biblical principle: to whom much is given, much is expected (Luke 12:48). In fact, the founding of the United States il-lustrates how Christian citizens should apply biblical prin-ciples to their government and encourage their leaders to uphold them.

THE AMERICAN EXPERIMENT

Our country has been blessed because in many areas, our founders applied godly principles, shaping the

American governance model according to those biblical values. God has honored the efforts of America's founders, blessing our nation with liberty and freedoms.

An obvious divergence from biblical principles, however, is America's commingling of antislavery and pro-slavery values, which combined with external factors to cause human chattel slavery to proliferate in the States, just as it had proliferated throughout European colonies and Africa for centuries prior. The founders wrote the Constitution and other contemporary documents, like the Northwest Ordinance of 1787 and the congressional ban of the international slave trade in 1808, so as to set slavery on what Lincoln later recognized as the path to "ultimate extinction":

> The Union is a house divided against itself ... I agree to the fact, and I account for it by looking at the position in which our fathers originally placed it—restricting it from the new Territories where it had not gone, and legislating to cut off its source by the abrogation of the slave-trade[,] thus putting the seal of legislation *against its spread*. The public mind *did* rest in the belief that it was in the course of ultimate extinction.... Now, I believe if we could arrest the spread, and place it where Washington, and Jefferson, and Madison placed it, it *would be* in the course of ultimate extinction.[4]

Tragically, Eli Whitney's invention of the cotton gin in 1793—six years after the Constitution was drafted—made the perpetuation of human chattel slavery too lucrative a temptation for many civil leaders and citizens to resist. From this, violence and injustice have flowed through much of our nation's history—and this evil has been inadequately opposed. Through this disobedience, we see that the blessings of liberty and freedom naturally fade when nations stray from biblical principles.

In America's history, we see injustice clearly in issues like slavery or in the holocaust of abortion. These injustices are sinful—they are wrong, and God's word declares them to be wrong. Scripture commands us to speak up for the innocent and protect those who cannot protect themselves (Exod. 23:2; Prov. 24:11–12, 31:8; Hab. 1:13). Out of duty to God's kingdom, we condemn the injustice of abortion and seek to expose it as wicked (Exod. 20:13; Job 31:15; Ps. 127:3–5, 139:13–16). The same was true for slavery; while certainly there were Christians who practiced slavery, the Bible is clear that man-stealing is condemned (Exod. 21:16; Deut. 24:7) and those who practiced it ought to have had no place in the church (1 Tim. 1:10). Slavery may have been legal in the City of Man, but it was incompatible with the City of God—and Christians were to work to expose it as evil and call people to repentance. Those are just two of many examples of how Christians can influence life in the City of Man, without claiming that the City of Man should be ruled by the church.

Christians can confront and expose sin effectively because we acknowledge the existence of an authoritative God, the reality of universal truth, and the standard of right versus wrong. This belief is not reserved for Sunday school curriculum. It is evident in America's Declaration of Independence. You can't say "all men are created equal" if you don't believe that all men are *created*. You cannot say "all men are created" if you don't believe that there's a Creator. And if you disbelieve in a Creator, you cannot logically believe that right and wrong exist. You cannot be a powerful force to expose what is immoral and affirm what is good without a robust system of ethics flowing from divine revelation.

HOW THE KINGDOMS ADVANCE

It is axiomatic that nations rise and fall. Borders change. Populations grow. In one sense, this is true not only of nations but also for the church. The basic idea that the kingdom of God can advance on earth is essential to the doctrine of two kingdoms taught by Jesus.

Think of how nations advance: they annex other areas, they tax, and they force compliance. A good nation expands by checking evil and advancing freedoms. Wicked nations advance too—by conquering and subjugating. God's kingdom advances altogether differently. The kingdom of God advances when souls are added to the church through personal conversion. A basic new-covenant reality is that a person cannot be forced to come to faith in Christ against his or her will, but only when God *changes* his or her will. The kingdom of God grows one person at a time, and it grows when a person is freely converted—when the Spirit of God works in an individual's heart and changes his or her desires, so that he or she bends a knee to Christ.

Conversion cannot be legislated—though some have tried. For example, Constantine marched multitudes at sword point through the waters of baptism. In his mind, he was growing the kingdom of God by growing his earthly kingdom. He assumed that since he ruled both cities, each person who was added to his earthly empire was added to God's empire as well.

But the New Testament confirms God's kingdom doesn't function that way. Jesus did not die for nations; he died for individual souls. For that reason, it is misguided to call any nation a *Christian nation*, even if its governing principles are biblically based. When the New Testament speaks of nations, it refers to them a place where the gospel is preached (Rom. 1:5; 1 Tim. 3:16). It does not refer to *nations* themselves being "Christian." Nations cannot be saved or baptized; only individuals can. Conformity to the image of Christ comes as the kingdom of God advances through conversion, not as God's people redeem culture or advance a political agenda in the City of Man.

BELIEVERS IN THE WORLDLY KINGDOM

How should believers—citizens of heaven—relate to the government of the earthly nation of which they are citizens? Jesus answers this question in Matthew 22:16–22. But before we look at that passage, let's review its context.

Matthew 22 is set up by Mathew 21:33–46, in which Jesus tells a familiar parable about a landowner who leased a vineyard to tenant farmers. At harvest, he sent his officials to collect the rent. The tenants refused to pay, beating up the officials instead. He sent more, and they were mistreated as well. Finally, the landowner sent his son, whom the tenants murdered. Jesus compared the murderous tenants to the Pharisees who were plotting his crucifixion—and he predicted their destruction.

In the next passage, Matthew 22:1–14, Jesus shares another parable about a wedding feast that a king prepared for his son. The king asked his servants to call the invited guests to come to the feast. Those invited to be guests refused—and killed the servants. In his anger, the king sent troops to destroy the murderers and burn their city. Jesus's point here was clear: the destruction of the religious leaders was forthcoming.

The Pharisees could not tolerate Jesus any longer, and they crafted a plot to entrap him. They wanted him to say something that contradicted the Torah or that revealed a threat to Rome, so they planned to trick Jesus with a series of three questions from three different groups. Each question was clever, complicated, and, in a sense, timeless.

The first ambush was what this entire book is about: the relationship of believers and government. The second was about the resurrection—which the Sadducees denied—and the third was about the hierarchy of importance of certain regulations within the Torah. All three questions still apply today, but the remainder of this chapter focuses on the first, and it fills out our understanding of why Christians are to respect, obey, and sometimes resist civil authority.

ET TU, BRUTE?

Matthew 22 (paralleled in Mark 12) recounts the challenging conversation. Matthew 22:16 states, "So, they [the Pharisees] sent their disciples to him along with the Herodians [a group of Jews who were loyal to Herod] saying, 'Teacher, we know that you are true and teach the way of God truthfully.'"

These Pharisees and Herodians were hypocrites. When they claimed, "Teacher, we know that you are true," they were either lying or condemning themselves. If they really knew Jesus spoke the truth, then why would they try to "trap him" in his words? Yet in God's providence, Jesus let them ask the questions even though he knew their motive.

They asked Jesus, "Is it lawful to pay taxes to Caesar or not?" (Matt. 22:17). That is a harder question than it appears on the surface. Why did they ask it? Was it a question about appropriate taxation rates? Were the Pharisees and Herodians big-government spenders who wanted to fuel vast entitlement programs?

As the establishment party, the Pharisees wanted to preserve the status quo, including their position of power. The Herodians partnered with the Pharisees in their opposition to Jesus. Both groups assumed that if he really were the Messiah, he would likely overthrow Roman rule. And if Roman rule fell, the Pharisees were sure to lose their temple and Herodians would likely lose their lives. By AD 33, the Pharisees and Herodians were unlikely allies, united in their need for stable Roman rule.

Their logic made sense: Jesus had cleansed the temple the week before, so in their minds, he had his sights on a revolution. They were determined to turn Rome—or at least the Jewish crowd—against him.

Inciting the crowd to oppose Jesus was no small undertaking. As Jews, the crowd despised paying the Roman tax. The Romans believed Caesar was a god and required people to pay their taxes with a particular coin, one that had Caesar's image on it. Possessing a coin with the image of a false god on its face forced Jews to violate the second commandment. Every time they paid the tax, Jews were reminded of Roman occupation, and they despised Rome for requiring a coin that flagrantly mocked their Torah.

The situation was even more complex, because the Roman Empire had recently ended a Jewish rebellion in Israel. Herod the Great had gotten Israel to cooperate with Roman rule by building the Jews a temple. They were allowed to have their own form of Jewish worship with their own currency and sacrifices. The tradeoff was that they had to use the Roman coin, with Caesar's image, for the Roman tax.

But the coin's more immediate problem was much deeper than the image. The coin read, "Tiberius, Caesar Augustus, son of the divine Augustus." This statement elevated him to divine status, contrary to God's law, which says, "You shall have no other gods before me" (Exod. 20:3). In this way, the coin forced Jews to violate the first *and* second commandments! Jesus was being asked if Jews should even possess such an idolatrous coin. If he said, "No, don't pay your taxes," then he would be in open rebellion against Rome. But if he said, "Yes, pay your taxes," he would be endorsing having idolatrous coins in their purses.

Jesus's standing as a Galilean also added difficulty to the question. Galileans were exempt from paying the tax, so if his answer encouraged the crowd to pay the tax, he might win the Pharisees but come across as out of touch with the common people.

Thus, their question, "Is it right to pay the imperial tax to Caesar or not?" was loaded. The Herodians, ever loyal to Rome and seeing no problem in paying their taxes, had set the trap for Jesus with one question. While it looks like a question about the Roman tax, this question points to the intersection of the City of Man and the City of God.

Jesus spotted the malicious intent of their entrap- ment and answered in a way that masterfully described the citizen of heaven's relationship to earthly kingdoms. Here is the exchange:

> Tell us, then, what you think. Is it lawful to pay taxes to Caesar, or not? But Jesus, aware of their malice, said, "Why put me to the test, you hypocrites? Show me the coin for the tax." And they brought him a denarius. And Jesus said to them, "Whose likeness and inscription is this?" They said, "Caesar's." Then he said to them, "Therefore render to Caesar the things that are Caesar's, and to God the things that are God's." When they heard it, they marveled. And they left him and went away. (Matt. 22:17–22).

In other words, Jesus declared it right and lawful for them to give the coin back to Caesar, because it literally had his picture on it. *It belongs to him, so you can go ahead and give it to him.* Jesus had deftly navigated the trap. He neither embraced idolatry nor nullified the second commandment. Instead, he charted a course for the citizen of heaven to live as a citizen of earth. Jesus was endorsing a principle that extends to our era: in essence, some things belong to the government, so we can give them to the government.

TO CAESAR WHAT IS CAESAR'S

Jesus had the authority to tell the Jews to pay taxes to Rome, and he has the authority to tell us the same thing. The first few verses of Romans 13 take Jesus's principle—give to government what belongs to government—and detail what belongs to it: obedience (v. 1), submission (v. 2), and taxes (v. 6). Paul even says to honor and respect our political leaders: "Pay to all what is owed to them: taxes to whom taxes are owed, revenue to whom revenue is owed, respect to whom respect is owed, honor to whom honor is owed" (Rom. 13:7).

This message echoes in his first letter to the young pastor Timothy:

> First of all, then, I urge that supplications, prayers, intercessions, and thanksgivings be made for all people, for kings and all who are in high positions, that we may lead a peaceful and quiet life, godly and dignified in every way (1 Tim. 2:1–2).

God designed all nations with the purpose to check evil and promote good. All citizens should be thankful for their country and should be submissive to its laws, pay its taxes, and honor its leaders. If we are not paying taxes or show-ing gratitude for our governmental leaders and for the country we live in, we are sinning.

This does not mean—nor does Jesus's answer im-ply—that we should pay as much in taxes as we can. In fact, wise stewardship demands that we lower our tax lia-bility within the boundaries of the law. But Jesus's answer to the Herodians does mean that Christians should never shirk their legitimate tax burden by playing fast and loose with tax law or making unlawful claims concerning what we owe. Christians should not cheat on their taxes. Today, most currency is manufactured by the government. Amer-ican currency says on it, "In God we trust," but above our national motto, it says, "United States of America." In that sense, the very currency in your purse or wallet belongs to the government. Go ahead and give it back to your civil leaders when they lawfully ask for it.

God allows people to earn money in this world and then steward that money for our good and for his glory. We can use the treasure God gives us to provide for our fami-lies, invest wisely, enjoy the fruits of our labors, give relief to the poor, and send missionaries into the world. All of this takes place in the context of a taxation system, where our country has a claim on a portion of our income. So, when government lawfully requires our money, we need to give it back.

TO GOD WHAT IS GOD'S

Did you notice that we explored only the "Render to Caesar the things that are Caesar's" half of Jesus's answer? He went on to teach that, in contrast to currency, worship does not belong to the government. True to the matchless rabbi he was, Jesus turned the lesson on taxation into a spiritual challenge. The antagonists asked about giving the tax coin to Caesar, with no mention of their obligations to give to God. Jesus's answer took them deeper, where they did not want to go.

Jesus extended the lesson in this way: we owe the government our taxes, civic loyalty, thankfulness, and prayers—but we owe God something else. We owe God our affections, hearts, and worship. Really, everything we have belongs to God. But what he has in mind here is the religious affections of the heart. The Lord doesn't need your sacrifices, but he demands an obedient and contrite spirit (Ps. 51:17)—something many Jews in the first century were unwilling to give. Jesus called their bluff, and they simply walked away.

The Pharisees and Herodians pretended that their problem lay in rendering what they should give to Caesar. Their real problem, though, was their refusal to render to God what is God's. The greatest commandment is, after all, to love the Lord your God with all your heart, soul, and mind (Matt. 22:37). They feigned concern about withholding taxes when their real issue was their withholding of worship.

Though we live in the City of Man, we worship in the City of God. When Jesus said, "Render to Caesar the things that are Caesar's and to God the things that are God's" (Matt. 22:21), the Pharisees were astonished. They thought they had boxed Jesus in, but he escaped their trap. They "marveled" and, for a few more days, they left him alone (Matt. 22:22). Later, when they brought Jesus to trial, they falsely accused him of saying that people shouldn't pay taxes to Caesar! (Luke 23:2).

DUAL CITIZENSHIP

If the Jews thought Jesus was going to overthrow Rome, they were mistaken. On the heels of clearing the temple of the money changers, Jesus did not merely steer clear of a Roman uprising—he validated Rome's civil authority over his fellow Jews. This crushed the spirits of some of the Jewish leaders. Even the disciples might have been disappointed to find out that Jesus was not going to liberate them from Rome (cf. Luke 24:21; Acts 1:6). Instead of liberating Israel, Jesus showed up at the temple and instructed them to pay their taxes. How divinely ironic!

The disciples lacked a grid for understanding how these two kingdoms—the City of Man and the City of God—could possibly operate together. They stumbled over Jesus's prediction of the temple's destruction (Matt. 24:2). Jesus prophesied that their religious oversight as well as their beloved temple would be destroyed brick by brick (Matt. 24:2). They were going to lose both their nation and their religion (Matt. 21:43).

The kingdom "would be taken from" the Jewish leaders, and it would "be given to another people producing its fruits" (Matt. 21:43). This new people would not reclaim the earthly temple, nor would they relaunch temple worship. In fact, they wouldn't be headquartered in Israel at all. Instead, God's plan would send citizens of his kingdom into all the world, and they would be citizens of many different nations (Matt. 24:9, 14, 28:19; Acts 1:8, 2:9–12, 14:16). Just as God intended, the church has expanded into the whole world (Matt. 28:19). It is worth noting that the expansion of the church did not occur through political influence. It came by calling people to repent and believe the gospel. As the designer of this plan, Jesus bid the proud Pharisees not only to pay their dues to Caesar but also to pay their dues to God. Instead of setting loyalty to God and loyalty to Caesar in opposition, Jesus elevated loyalty to both.

Today, every Christian is part of two kingdoms, and Christ is Lord of them both. But he does rule them by different means, and neither kingdom rules the other. The government does not have authority over the church, and the church does not have authority over the government. They coexist—and when properly functioning, one does not pose a threat to the other. Christian belief does not interfere with a citizen's obedience to civil power functioning within God's design.

Earthly government ruling by God's design warrants our submission. If the government forbids you from doing something the Bible commands, you should disobey the government and honor God. If the government inter-feres with how the church should worship, the church has—by God's design—the right and responsibility to dis-obey the government and honor God. But those exceptions are rare in America. Even in the Roman Empire, Jesus urged submission to both kingdoms.

We recognize that the future kingdom of God is not revealed on earth yet. When Jesus returns, the two king-doms will become one. In the meantime, we wait for Je-sus's return as citizens of heaven and citizens of the United States. One of those citizenships is eternal; the other is not. We cannot look to government for our sense of secu-rity, direction, or purpose. Misdirected hope in government says, "Unless we do this, that, or the other, our nation will fall, and all hope will be lost." Nonsense. Nations rise and fall by the sovereign will of God. Hope doesn't belong to government.

In contrast, our hope in God will never fail. Scrip-ture says our eternal city is one that "cannot be shaken," so we should look for our hope in the City of God, not in the City of Man (Heb. 12:27).

WHERE DO WE GO FROM HERE?

Scripture makes it clear that we live in the here and now, waiting and praying for God's kingdom to come. Not everything we do is advancing the kingdom of God, but everything we do should be obedient to the Lord of both kingdoms. Do some soul searching right now.

- Have you placed your hope in your government or in your God?

- Have you faithfully paid your taxes honestly and with integrity?

- Have you prayed for the elected leaders God has put in place—even if you did not vote for them?

The church today faces temptations to render to the government things that belong only to God. As government grows, our society increasingly looks to it for meaning—in a sense, our society deifies government. We look to it to right wrongs, to punish the wicked, and to reward the righteous. We are like the Roman world in which Augustine wrote *The City of God.* We think that the rise and fall of government is an indication of our faithfulness to God. We act as if all hope for future generations is lost when our government falters.

But the truth is God did not design government to give eternal meaning and purpose to life. While it is certainly meant to check evil, there is only so much it can do. God alone can right every wrong and punish every wicked deed. God alone can wipe away every tear, and God alone can give hope and meaning in a world filled with wrong.

Thus, the church today has the same call that Augustine gave to his readers and the same call that the Puritans gave to their congregants. We are to turn to the Father, Son, and Spirit for meaning and direction. We are to rely on God's word to fuel our life—not on the government. In short, we are to "render to God the things that are God's."

[1] Augustine, *The City of God* 5.22.

[2] Augustine, *The City of God* 5.33.

[3] "Boniface VIII, The Bull Unam Sanctam (1302)," http://media.bloomsbury.com/rep/files/primary-source-39-boniface-unam-sanctam.pdf.

[4] Abraham Lincoln, "First Debate: Ottawa, Illinois," The Lincoln-Douglas Debates of 1858, August 21, 1858, National Park Service, https://www.nps.gov/liho/learn/historyculture/debate1.htm.

ABOUT THE AUTHOR

Jesse Johnson is the dean of The Master's Seminary in Washington, DC. He pastors Immanuel Bible Church in Springfield, Virginia, and is a trustee of The Master's University in Los Angeles, California.

He has degrees from The University of New Mexico (BA in Sociology and Spanish) and The Master's Seminary (MDiv and ThM in theology), and he is a current PhD student at Christ College in Sydney, Australia.

Jesse is the editor of *Evangelism* in the John MacArthur pastoral library series, published by Thomas Nelson. He teaches theology and evangelism at The Master's Seminary and formerly was a chaplain for the Los Angeles County Sheriff's department.

Jesse and his wife, Deidre, live in the Washington, DC, area with their three children, Madison, Savannah, and Geneva.

You can follow his writing at thecripplegate.com.

NOTE ON THE TEXT

The idea of this book, like much its text, germinated as a four-part sermon series the author preached at Immanuel Bible Church in Springfield, Virginia, in November and December 2020. An editorial team transcribed the sermon audio and, in close consultation with the author, reduced, restructured, and revised the text, adding to and subtracting from its pages to optimize its argument, keeping in mind that what proves rhetorically effective for teaching from the pulpit is not always rhetorically effective for teaching through a book, and vice versa.

The pivot in medium from a sermon series to a book with chapters does not, however, imply a great shift in audience. Although writing for consumption and application by the universal church in any country or era, the author and editor have intended the primary beneficiary of this teaching to be the author's own congregation. This is because it is impossible to conceive of "the church" obeying God's word apart from individual saints doing so. God's design is that these individual saints gather together in close, accountable community to receive and apply the faithful teaching of God's word by qualified elders, use their God-given gifts to edify their local number, and practice Christ's love toward each other and to unbelievers.

The intent regarding audience is further congruent with the editorial program that guided this book's conversion from a sermon series—Sermon TRANSCENSION: Transcription for 21st-Century Churches℠—the mission

of which is to help pastors shepherd their local congregations by extending and deepening the impact of their ser-
mons.

Should God use this book's teaching to equip saints
beyond this initial audience, as one hopes he will, let that
and all things be to his glory.

— Michael T. Hamilton,
CEO, Good Comma Editing
Founder, Sermon TRANSCENSIONᔆᔐ